Praise for *Heavy Hitter Sales Wisdom*

"It's difficult to find published sales strategies that go beyond simply reminding you of what you already know. However, *Heavy Hitter Sales Wisdom* forces readers to reevaluate their own strategy, tactics, persuasion, and sales common sense."

> —Bob Hughes, Executive Vice President,
> Global Sales, Services, and Marketing,
> Akamai Technologies, Inc.

"*Heavy Hitter Sales Wisdom* is a practical solution selling guide, loaded with real-world analogies, personal experiences, and modern proof points sure to enhance the success rate of anybody selling large complex solutions."

> —James Lewandowski, Executive Vice
> President of the Americas, McAfee

"*Heavy Hitter Sales Wisdom* provides innovative insight and inspiration for anyone who practices the art and science of sales."

> —Scott Raskin,
> Chief Executive Officer, Mindjet

"A great overview of strategic selling processes captured through the effective use of history, interesting anecdotes, and personal reflections, *Heavy Hitter Sales Wisdom* will be appreciated by novice salespeople as well as experienced Heavy Hitters."

> —Steven Blum, Vice President,
> Americas Sales, Autodesk, Inc.

"*Heavy Hitter Sales Wisdom* provides sales adrenaline and reinforces the skills required to win new clients and defeat competitors."

> —Stephen A. DeBacco, Chief Operating
> Officer, Workbrain Inc.

"*Heavy Hitter Sales Wisdom* goes beyond the nice-guy limitations of most sales books to define sales as what it really is—corporate warfare. It is a must-read for sales organizations that want to turn their sales forces into fire-breathing sales warriors."

—Jon Hanson, Vice President, Sales,
Cornerstone OnDemand, Inc.

"Reading *Heavy Hitter Sales Wisdom* is the easy way to learn where the 'mines' in the selling 'minefield' are versus the hard knocks of experience."

—Mark Milford, Senior Vice President,
Worldwide Sales and Support,
BakBone Software

"*Heavy Hitter Sales Wisdom* captures the essence of complex selling and provides the reader a road map to success. The use of military history and terms and tactics allows the reader to grasp what he or she *must* do in order to win the sale."

—Conal E. Finnegan, Vice President
Sales and Marketing, Purolator USA Inc.

"Anyone who thinks sales is about working harder, listen up! It's about working smarter. *Heavy Hitter Sales Wisdom* is not another 'do it' book. It is a 'get it' book. Sales success is all about how you think."

—Jim Panoff, Executive Vice President,
Sales and Marketing, Spheris

"The biggest challenge salespeople face is taking their skills to the next level. *Heavy Hitter Sales Wisdom* reduces the time it takes to become a Heavy Hitter."

> —Christopher Olsen, District Vice President,
> Sales, Graybar

"*Heavy Hitter Sales Wisdom* brings a fresh new approach to the solution selling environment. It offers stimulating ideas and sales strategies from captivating stories of battle and war that will help Heavy Hitters close more business."

> —Greg Gadbois, Executive Vice President,
> Sales, Service Net

"*Heavy Hitter Sales Wisdom* provides a comparison between the strategies of war and sales that is very different. Its insight to winning sales strategies and proven persuasion secrets make it a must-read for any veteran sales warrior."

> —Zach Bawel, Vice President of Sales,
> Jasper Engines & Transmissions

"The beauty of this book is the 'wisdom' it provides that can be applied to all aspects of our lives—and should be."

> —Earle Zucht, Senior Vice President, Sales,
> LogicalApps

"Finally, someone has explained the 'essence' of the Heavy Hitters—those who make it look so natural and easy."

> —Morton Mackof, Executive Vice President,
> Sales, EDGAR Online, Inc.

"Steve's wisdom pushes sellers to get out of the traditional selling model and directs them to seek mutual value, focusing on the political reality and objective criteria of the selling decision."

—Pete Van Sistine, Senior Vice President
of Sales and Marketing, Metavante

"Winning the competitive battle for customers takes more than reciting product features and functions. It takes a well-thought-out strategy, persuasive arguments, and common-sense sales execution—all of which can be found in *Heavy Hitter Sales Wisdom*."

—Peter Riccio, Vice President,
SuccessFactors

HEAVY HITTER SALES WISDOM

Proven Sales Warfare Strategies, Secrets of Persuasion, and Common-Sense Tips for Success

STEVE W. MARTIN

WILEY

John Wiley & Sons, Inc.

To salespeople, the modern-day warriors of the business world:
Seek, conquer, celebrate

For general information on our other products and services or for technical support, please contact our Customer Care Department within the United States at (800) 762-2974, outside the United States at (317) 572-3993 or fax (317) 572-4002.

Wiley also publishes its books in a variety of electronic formats. Some content that appears in print may not be available in electronic books. For more information about Wiley products, visit our web site at www.wiley.com.

Library of Congress Cataloging-in-Publication Data:

Martin, Steve W., 1960–
    Heavy hitter sales wisdom : proven sales warfare strategies, secrets of persuasion, and common-sense tips for success / Steve W. Martin.
        p.   cm.
    Includes bibliographical references and index.
    ISBN-13: 978-0-470-05231-0 (cloth)
    ISBN-10: 0-470-05231-7 (cloth)
    1. Selling.   2. Business communication.   3. Success in business.   I. Title.
    HF5438.25.M37365   2006
    658.85—dc22

                                                                2006009964

Printed in the United States of America.

10   9   8   7   6   5   4   3   2   1

Contents

Strategy, Persuasion, and Common Sense— the Three Parts of Sales Wisdom

> Glory is fleeting, but obscurity is forever.
> —NAPOLEON BONAPARTE

All salespeople must play three completely different roles to succeed. First, they must be generals who create a strategy to win their wars long before the first battle begins. The successful military leader painstakingly plans how and where he will attack in accordance with the troops and weapons at his disposal. When the fighting starts, the commander who will be victorious achieves his objective through battlefield maneuvers to gain the advantage and through countertactics to neutralize his enemy's advance.

Second, all salespeople must be professional persuaders. In essence, salespeople are paid to persuade. They must gain the willing obedience of others and convince complete strangers to follow their advice. However, the most product-knowledgeable salesperson is not necessarily the most persuasive one. Persuasive salespeople naturally connect with customers, instill customer confidence, and establish trust.

Finally, successful salespeople must be oracles who predict their chances of winning based on their common-sense judgment. As common sense accumulates over the years through interactions with customers, it becomes a salesperson's lifesaving device. It prevents salespeople from repeating past mistakes and guides their intuition to maximize their most precious resource: time.

When a salesperson has mastered these three roles—strategist, persuader, and common-sense sage—he or she has attained sales wisdom and become a Heavy Hitter. Heavy Hitters are truly great salespeople who have acquired prominence through their accomplishments, expertise, and judgment. They continually exceed quotas, close big deals, and enjoy themselves in the process.

Heavy Hitter Sales Wisdom takes the concept of becoming a Heavy Hitter to the next level. This book has been written for senior salespeople, those who have been in the field for 5, 10, and 15 years or more. While it will expose the novice salesperson to entirely new aspects of selling, the ultimate goal of *Heavy Hitter Sales Wisdom* is to help experienced salespeople expand their influence within their local office, region, sales organization, and company. This requires not only winning more business but also having a methodology to explain to others how and why you win.

Heavy Hitter Sales Wisdom is also in an entirely different category of sales book. Almost all of the many books about selling that are available today can be classified into one of two categories. The first category oversimplifies the complexity of selling. These books present sales in a very basic and simple way, seemingly aimed at those just beginning a career in sales. One common critique of these lightweight books is that they present common knowledge and fundamental concepts that almost everyone in sales already knows. They don't offer any innovative tactics or advanced sales techniques for old pros.

The second category takes a textbook-type approach to sales. These books concentrate on the logical and procedural aspects of the sales cycle. They focus on prospecting and qualifying, and they include formulaic concepts that the salesperson commits to memory. They don't take into account the human nature of sales and how people and politics determine account strategy. Although these books offer detailed information, they are laborious to read. The reader must sift through the entire book to gain a morsel of enlightenment.

Heavy Hitter Sales Wisdom does not fall into either of these categories. This book is intended to educate and enlighten experienced professionals on state-of-the-art sales strategies and entirely new philosophies about persuasion in an exciting and entertaining way. Equally important, *Heavy Hitter Sales Wisdom* provides models of salesperson and customer behavior that seasoned salespeople can use to explain what they do naturally to others within their company: colleagues, sales management, and other interested parties throughout the organization (such as marketing, engineering, and the CEO).

Heavy Hitter Sales Wisdom is best suited for salespeople who sell complex enterprise products and solutions. In these deals, salespeople must penetrate large organizations, influence key decision makers, and dovetail their products' benefits to customers' internal politics. In order to win, they must build relationships with sophisticated buyers in different departments all across a company. They have to persuade people to believe in their solution at all levels of the organization, from the nine-to-fiver to midlevel management and the executive staff. Finally, they compete against wily competitors who are equipped with similar products and equal sales acumen.

Senior salespeople know that sales cannot be taught; sales must be learned. The rookie learns how to sell by riding along on sales calls with a more experienced representative. Junior salespeople add to their repertoire by emulating a veteran. Meanwhile, veterans hone their skills by watching senior deal makers, most likely from the ranks of management. Regardless of experience, all salespeople need mentors to improve their skills and become Heavy Hitters, because learning from a successful practitioner is the best way to learn anything new.

The term *heavy hitter* originated in the sport of boxing, where it literally meant "hitting hard," and has been transferred to people across all walks of life everywhere around the world. Today, accomplished sports heroes, politicians, entertainers, lawyers, doctors, and businesspeople are known as Heavy Hitters.

Heavy Hitter Sales Wisdom is based on the study of prominent Heavy Hitters throughout the ages. The Heavy Hitters included in this book are people of great influence who had a tremendous impact on our world. We will seek to understand how they rose to prominence, won their battles, and persuaded people to follow them. We want to learn from their successes and failures in order to become wiser ourselves.

This book includes comments from a diverse group of history's greatest Heavy Hitters, but we will study six leaders in greater detail to understand the skills they used to change the course of human history. What can salespeople learn from Sun Tzu, Napoleon Bonaparte, and George Patton? Why would studying the words of Buddha, Jesus Christ, and Ronald Reagan be important? Since learning by example is the most effective way to learn, we want to study role models who provide the best examples of strategy, persuasion, and common sense.

In the first part of the book we will study a fascinating subject with many parallels to sales: war. Strategies to win wars and close deals share many similar characteristics. Therefore, the first step in our pursuit of sales wisdom is to study the grand strategy of war. We will review different battlefield scenarios and examine the philosophies of three of the greatest war strategists of all time: Sun Tzu, Napoleon Bonaparte, and George Patton.

More than 2,500 years ago, Chinese general Sun Tzu wrote *The Art of War*, the most important book on war philosophy ever published. The premise of *The Art of War* is that successful warfare is based on having better information than the enemy by using spies, possessing the knowledge of when to fight, and attacking enemies where they are weakest and least expect it. Each of these mantras is equally applicable to sales.

Both U.S. Army General George S. Patton and Emperor of

France Napoleon Bonaparte were lifelong students of war. Both were devotees of the psychology of warfare. Each was a voracious reader of military history and had an encyclopedic knowledge of warfare. At the age of 16, Napoleon commanded a French army artillery garrison. By the age of 27 he commanded an entire army, and a few years later he had conquered Europe.

Nearly 125 years after Napoleon's death, General Patton would fight his way across France during World War II. Patton was described by Russian leader Joseph Stalin as the United States' best general. When a German senior officer was captured, he said, "General Patton is the most feared general on all fronts. The tactics of the general are daring and unpredictable. General Patton is always the main topic of conversation. Where is he? When will he attack? Where? How? With what?"[1]

I'd like to forewarn you that the sales strategy section includes detailed analysis of battles from a cross section of mankind's worst wars. These battlefield descriptions are more than just interesting anecdotes about military history. It's important to review the specific circumstances—who had the advantage, how the attack was planned, and when and where they fought—in order to understand who won and why. As you read them, pay particular attention to who were the underdogs, why they were at a disadvantage, and how the momentum of the battle was changed, because all of the facets of warfare that determine the victor and vanquished are directly applicable to salespeople who must invade new accounts or fend off competitors' attacks.

Unlike in a real war, salespeople fight with words, and in Part Two we will study three of the world's most persuasive people of all time: Buddha, Ronald Reagan, and Jesus Christ. At the age of 29 in 594 B.C., Siddhartha Gautama gave up his life of luxury to become a monk known as Buddha. He would spend the rest of his life learning the path to enlightenment by understanding the nature of reality and the importance of mental orientation through liberating one's spirit. Buddha's teachings were passed down from generation to generation in over five thousand volumes. Today, these teachings influence the daily lives of more than half a billion practicing Buddhists.

Another prominent persuader who impacted the world as we know it today was Ronald Reagan. In 2004, Ronald Reagan was named by an independent pollster as the third greatest American president of all time, behind Franklin Roosevelt and John Kennedy.[2] It's not surprising that he was ranked just behind these two national heroes. However, what made this president truly unique was his ability to communicate and persuade. In fact, Reagan is known in the annals of history as "the Great Communicator." Not only was he able to convince ordinary Americans that he was one of them, but equally important, the eloquent orator was able to influence adversarial lawmakers on Capitol Hill.

The fact that one-third of the six billion people on the planet follow the teachings of Jesus Christ is profound proof of the impact of his words. Obviously, his legacy continues to affect people all around the world daily. In addition, six billion copies of the Bible have been printed, making it the best-selling book of all time.

Since the premise of this book is modeling the most influential people of all time, we want mentors who have experienced a wide range of communication challenges, dealt with very skeptical audiences, and changed people's opinions under the most difficult circumstances. Jesus Christ clearly fits these requirements.

The communication methods of Buddha, Reagan, and Jesus are well worth studying today by those who must speak for a living and persuade others to believe in them. While thousands of books have been written from theological and political perspectives about these men, we are more interested in how and why they said something, rather than what they actually said. Therefore, we want to study and understand the purpose, content, and structure of their language to help us learn how to become more persuasive.

In the book's final part we will review the common sense of selling. We need common sense to reach our destination of success.

This part is organized differently from the others. It is composed primarily of what I call "metaphors"—stories, parables, and analogies that communicate ideas by using examples that people can relate to and identify with. Metaphors enable complex concepts and theories to be explained in a simple and understandable manner. Most interestingly, a metaphor is a single story that can convey many meanings.

The stories in Part Three cover a broad range of sales-related topics and come from a surprising array of sources, ranging from scientific journals to classified ads. These stories are grouped into lessons about sales and the life of a salesperson. They are much like the tales salespeople recount to each other at their favorite watering holes. Much can be learned from these stories, and they provide valuable common-sense wisdom.

Most people have misconceptions about what wisdom is. They think of wisdom as a serene, passive intelligence shaped by a lifetime of experiences. They believe wisdom is a natural part of aging. They associate wisdom with the old hermit who sequesters himself on a mountaintop. That's not my idea of wisdom. Wisdom is gained through your experiences in dealing with other people. Your wisdom increases daily as you navigate the path of life, regardless of your age. Wisdom can also be used proactively to shape the events that surround you.

While *Heavy Hitter Sales Wisdom* is the name of this book, it is also a very particular type of wisdom. All salespeople accumulate sales wisdom through interactions with customers, competitors, colleagues, and managers. Whenever salespeople risk defeat, they grow wiser. Heavy Hitter sales wisdom grows anytime salespeople are challenged in a trial by fire. Wherever salespeople beat the odds and win, they gain Heavy Hitter sales wisdom.

The dictionary defines "wisdom" as "follow[ing] the soundest course of action based upon knowledge."[3] Heavy Hitter sales wisdom is best described as "the knowledge that enables you to defeat your enemy by winning over the customer." Three equal parts form Heavy Hitter sales wisdom: sales strategy, persuasion, and common sense. We apply these three sales essentials together in a proactive, aggressive manner in order to win over customers, defeat our competitors, and advance our careers to the next level.

Sales is much more than a career. It is a lifestyle and a way of thinking. Selling is a mental, emotional, and spiritual profession that becomes a core part of the person who chooses it. While most of the world's professions have many gray areas, sales is a black-or-white profession. In sales, you either win or lose; there is nothing in between. Salespeople want to know the truth about their performance and, for that matter, themselves. Regardless of whether they have been selling for years or decades, they are in perpetual pursuit of personal validation.

Long-term salespeople also know they need an occasional shot of sales adrenaline to renew their sense of excitement. An underlying goal of *Heavy Hitter Sales Wisdom* is to uplift your spirits. Therefore, refer to it when you need mental refreshment or after a tough run of luck when you need to reanchor yourself to success. And while the wisdom in this book is aimed at making you a better salesperson, it will also make you a better person as a whole.

Heavy Hitter Sales Wisdom tells an adventure story about sales strategies, persuasion, and the common sense of selling by studying some of the most interesting and important people in history. Prepare yourself to relive your own wins and losses, learn something new, and be inspired by studying some of the world's all-time Heavy Hitters—because history can teach us many important lessons if we choose to listen.

PART ONE

Sales Warfare Strategies

SCIENTISTS BELIEVE that one of the major differences that separate human beings from the rest of the animal world is the fact that we wage war. Because war isn't instinctual, it is thought to be a uniquely human trait. It's something people choose to do.

If you are in sales, you are perpetually in a state of war. All sales-people are warriors who must fight the relentless march of time and enemies who are trying to defeat them daily. Sales is an intense hand-to-hand battle fought between two people or two groups of people who are each trying to win over the customer. The victor outsmarts, outmaneuvers, and overwhelms his enemies.

In sales, just as in war, there can be only one winner, and to-day's conqueror can quickly become tomorrow's vanquished. The deciding difference is strategy. Strategy is the most critical compo-nent of sales wisdom. Without the right sales strategy, persuasion and common sense are inconsequential. In this part we will study the grand strategy of war and three of the greatest war strategists of all time—Sun Tzu, Napoleon Bonaparte, and George Patton—to understand how they won and what the ages have to teach us about defeating our enemies on the battlefield of business sales.

CHAPTER 1

The Grand Strategy of War

He who exercises no forethought but makes light of his opponents is sure to be captured by them.

—SUN TZU
The Art of War

The Civil War was anything but civil, and on a hot summer day in July 1863, two massive armies set out to destroy one another. Approximately 75,000 men of the Confederate Army squared off against 80,000 Union troops in Gettysburg, Pennsylvania. After three days of fighting, one-third of these men would be killed, wounded, or captured in one of the Civil War's bloodiest battles.

Although the victory by the Union troops would become the war's turning point in terms of momentum and morale, the first day of the fighting was in fact won by General Robert E. Lee's Confederate forces. The battle started at 5:30 in the morning as a skirmish between forward units. It wasn't until noon that General Lee and the bulk of his army arrived on the field. Even though Lee was hesitant to engage in battle in unfamiliar territory and without knowing the strength of his enemy, he pressed his troops into action. Lee's decision was right, and by nightfall the Confederates had killed or captured 12,000 Union soldiers.

General George C. Meade's Union troops were facing a test. One month earlier, Lee's army had defeated them at Chancellorsville. Morale was sagging and they questioned their ability to win the war. They had to make a stand and prove they could win by stopping the marauding enemy from advancing northward. The

Union Army's strategy on the first day of the battle was simple. Since it was initially outnumbered nearly two to one, the plan was to delay Lee's army until more troops could be brought forward to the battleground from the rear. Although the Union troops lost the first day's contest numerically, they had accomplished their mission. They had stopped Lee's advance and, equally important, held the tactical terrain: the hills and high ground surrounding Gettysburg that provided the defenders with an important advantage.

Encouraged by his first day's results, Lee decided to take the offensive again on the second day of the battle. Meanwhile, the Union defenders made preparations for the anticipated attack, and more troops arrived overnight. While each army lost nine thousand men on the second day, in fighting that can best be described as a draw, the Union forces still held all their strategic positions.

Undaunted by the preceding day's results, Lee attacked once again on the third day of the battle. At 1:00 P.M., the Confederate artillery launched a massive barrage on the Union line. Nearly two miles away, the Union artillery responded in kind. For two hours more than 250 cannons dueled in a deafening roar of death, confusion, and chaos. A newspaper reporter on the scene said, "Every size and form of shell known to British and to American gunnery shrieked, whirled, moaned, whistled, and wrathfully fluttered over our ground. As many as six a second, constantly two in a second, bursting and screaming over and around the headquarters, made a very hell of fire that amazed the oldest officers."[1]

After the heavy exchange of cannon fire died down, Lee ordered Major General George Edward Pickett to attack the center of the Union line with his division. A Confederate officer said of the order at the time, "I don't want to make this attack. I believe it will fail. I do not see how it can succeed. I would not make it even now, but that Gen. Lee has ordered and expects it."[2] Pickett's men assembled and collected themselves. Some pinned notes onto themselves so they would be correctly identified in case of their demise.

In what is known as Pickett's charge, six thousand men marched across the shell-scarred battlefield, which resembled the moon more than a rural field in Pennsylvania. Fifty minutes later, half of them were killed, captured, or wounded before the survivors straggled back to the Confederate line. A Union soldier said of the suicidal attack, "The rebs were fallin' like wheat to a reaper."[3] Following the attack, when Lee asked about the status of his division, Pickett replied, "General, I have no division."[4] The attack was a catastrophe and effectively ended the three-day battle. Lee had lost the most decisive battle of the war.

Lee's attack at Gettysburg and Pickett's charge in particular are examples of the "direct strategy" of attack. The direct strategy is based on brute strength and the overwhelming of an enemy by sheer force. In every case, a direct attack is a collision that results in a cataclysmic culmination; one side is defeated by the other.

A direct attack has only two possible outcomes. First, the attackers may ransack the defenders and overtake their position. However, this is accomplished only when the attackers have far greater strength. The second outcome is by far the more likely of the two. The attackers will be repulsed and in the process lose their momentum and morale and be plunged into chaos. An unsuccessful direct attack disintegrates the attackers' overall ability to win the war. In the case of Pickett's charge, the frontal assault against a well-entrenched defender was, predictably, a disaster.

Through the millennia, the methods used to fight wars didn't change. For the better part of the past four hundred years, war was based upon the direct strategy. It was a test of courage as soldiers marched shoulder to shoulder to square off against their opponents in suicidal crossfire. However, as muskets gave way to machine guns, it became impossible to fight in this manner. The strategy of warring changed as the weaponry grew more sophisticated. In many respects, the nature of selling needs to undergo a similar evolution.

THE CHANGING NATURE
OF SALES

For the past two decades, selling has been conducted in basically the same way. Salespeople approach customers armed with facts, features, and specifications about their products to convince customers to buy. However, customer decision making has changed radically during this time frame. This incredible transformation is due to the changing nature of the customers themselves.

Today's customers are smarter and more sophisticated, and technology has become a way of life for them. For example, our cars have global positioning and mapping systems based on satellite communications. The appliances in our kitchens turn themselves on and off. Our entire music collections are carried on digital devices the size of a deck of cards. We take pictures, play games, and send text messages to friends with our cellular phones. Eighty percent of all homes in the United States have personal computers. Via the Internet, customers can research products, prices, and opinions. Collectively, this has raised the level of sophistication of the customers we must converse with and sell to.

Perhaps the most interesting change is how people receive information. According to one university study, the world's total yearly production of media content for newspapers, magazines, radio, television, and the Internet would require roughly 1.5 billion gigabytes of storage. This is the equivalent of 250 megabytes per person for each man, woman, and child on the earth.[5] Because of this information overload, customer attention spans are shorter than ever.

Information must now be packaged with the customers' shortened attention spans in mind. For example, *USA Today*, the largest-selling newspaper in the United States, was designed to stand out visually. The colorful newspaper always includes bold diagrams and numerous pictures so that time-pressed readers can pick up a story's message with minimal effort. Even the racks used to sell the newspaper are colorful boxes with rounded edges as op-posed to the black square boxes of other newspapers.

Shortened attention spans have changed the nature of information itself. *USA Today* distills and condenses the news into easy-to-read chunks. A paragraph is rarely longer than three short sentences. Every article is written with the reader in mind, using a "what's in it for me?" style. *USA Today*'s style is best summarized by the newspaper's tagline, "An economy of words, a wealth of information."[6] If imitation is the sincerest form of flattery, *USA Today* is the most successful newspaper ever, because newspapers everywhere have adopted its format.

Another media giant has had a tremendous influence on customers. While the term *MTV generation* might conjure images of *Beavis and Butthead*, Generation X buyers—those born between 1961 and 1981—have had a tremendous impact on buyers of all ages. First, more than the members of any generation before, they are immune to sales pitches. The generation that studied Watergate, watched the Iran-Contra hearings, and eavesdropped on the Monica Lewinsky affair not only questions authority but is wired to distrust it. Since the people grew up with satellite and cable television, they expect instant access, 24-hour availability, and a quick turnaround of information.

The orientation of customers has also changed. They're more self-accomplished and self-reliant. Not so long ago, a gas station attendant would pump your gas, a bank teller would handle your deposit, and you knew the owner of the corner bakery. Today, you pay by credit card at the pump and fill the tank yourself, you bank online, and you shop at gigantic warehouse superstores. Just a few years ago, you might have visited several computer stores to find the right personal computer. Now you can configure new computers online and have them shipped right to your front door. Times have changed, and each generation of buyers is more sophisticated than the last, rendering traditional sales thinking obsolete.

The consumer has more choices than ever. If you visit the local supermarket to buy peas, you will have to make a selection from 20 different choices (fresh, frozen, canned, and different brands). Even though more variety is available today, there is very little difference between products, whether the customer is selecting vegetables, computer software, financial investments, or heavy equipment. In other words, purchase decisions aren't clear-cut anymore because all the competing products share the same basic features, functions, and benefits. Product differentiation is at an all-time low.

Customer expectations, however, are higher than ever. Whether we turn on a light switch or a car's ignition or swipe our card at the convenience store, we expect it to work flawlessly. This way of thinking has invaded all aspects of our lives, including how we purchase products. Conversely, our high expectations mean we have a very low tolerance for anything but perfection. A few years ago, I was ecstatic to have dial-up computer access, even though it was slower than molasses. Today, I am easily irritated when my broadband connection is slightly slower than normal and incensed when it is down.

The popular sales methodologies of the past 20 years have not adjusted to these new models of customer behavior. They are formulaic and based on the concept of a funnel. For example, you were probably taught, like I was, that you had to make 200 cold calls in order to achieve 20 sales calls with the hope of closing 2 deals. Using these numbers, you would experience 198 defeats in order to get 2 wins. I remember how depressed I was when I was presented with this sales methodology because of all the rejection I would have to experience. In fact, this direct, brute-force method of selling produces mainly failures.

Over the years, I have seen salespeople use direct strategies with prospective customers with outcomes similar to that of Pickett's charge. Some salespeople would show up at sales calls without any forethought about what they were about to do. Others thought customers would select them if they provided a litany of reasons why they shouldn't use the competition's products. Still others attacked customers using PowerPoint presentations, behaving as if the recitation of their product presentation alone would result in a deal. Unfortunately, all of these strategies actually drove customers away.

All these factors—today's smarter customers and their shortened attention spans, the lack of product differentiation, and outdated sales tactics—necessitate a change in the basic underlying premise of sales. Sales success in today's times requires a new way of thinking about sales strategy. The question is, what is the right strategy for today's customer?

THE INDIRECT STRATEGY

To answer this question, we need to look at an entirely different way to wage war. The indirect strategy is based on intelligence, finesse, and the element of surprise, rather than frontal assault. This time-tested strategy involves understanding one's own abilities and concentrating resources on the enemy's weaknesses. Above all, the strategy truly appreciates the importance of time, momentum, and the role human nature plays in determining the winner. (In this context, "indirect" does not refer to deals that are sold through a partner or third party sales channel. While you may choose to use partners as a distribution channel to increase sales, doing so is not a sales strategy in itself.)

In 1954, famous war historian B. H. Liddell Hart detailed the indirect approach to war in his classic book, *Strategy*. In painstaking detail he described the superiority of the indirect strategy over the direct strategy, using examples throughout the history of warfare. He theorized that the outcome of every major war from Roman times through World War II could be attributed to the grand strategy the parties selected. The victors always chose to battle indirectly.

Liddell Hart argued that the indirect approach was not solely a war strategy but also one of the most influential philosophies of mankind. He explained how he came to think of the indirect strategy as something much bigger than an edict for war—seeing it as a philosophy with universal application: "When, in the course of studying a long series of military campaigns, I first came to perceive the superiority of the indirect over the direct approach, I was looking merely for light upon strategy. With deepened reflection, however I began to realize that the indirect approach had a much wider application—that it was a law of life in all spheres: a truth of philosophy."[7]

Liddell Hart came to the realization that the indirect strategy could be applied wherever opposition to a new idea exists. For example, he said, "The suggestion that there is a bargain to be secured is far more potent than any direct appeal to buy."[8]

He further commented on the persuasive nature of the indirect versus the direct approach: "The direct assault of new ideas provokes a stubborn resistance, thus intensifying the difficulty of producing a change of outlook. Conversion is achieved more easily and rapidly by unsuspected infiltration of a different idea or by an argument that turns the flank of instinctive opposition."[9]

According to Liddell Hart, the indirect approach is one of life's grandest strategies and its application is universal. "The indirect approach is as fundamental to the realm of politics as to the realm of sex," he said.[10] The indirect approach is ideal for convincing without confrontation and gaining the willing obedience of others. It's also an offensive strategy. When forced to fight, it involves using surprise, deception, intelligence, logic, and human nature to exploit the enemy's weaknesses.

The origins of the indirect war strategy can be traced back more than 2,500 years to the Chinese general Sun Tzu. He wrote in *The Art of War*, "Indirect tactics, efficiently applied, are as inexhaustible as Heaven and Earth, unending as the flow of rivers and streams; like the sun and moon, they end but to begin anew; like the four seasons, they pass away but to return once more."[11]

On the surface, it seems odd that a career military man and merciless warrior who once had a concubine beheaded for disobeying orders would describe his fundamental war philosophy in such poetic terms. However, a closer look at his imaginative description yields subtle clues about the nature of the indirect strategy.

Sun Tzu equated the indirect strategy to the natural universe: the sun, the moon, water, and the four seasons. All are unstoppable natural forces. The sun can't be stopped from rising, the moon continues endlessly on its path, the flow of water carves canyons of rock, and the seasons repeat year after year in a never-ending cycle. According to Sun Tzu, anyone who masters the indirect strategy is tapping into another natural power.

The elegance and beauty with which Sun Tzu spoke of the indirect strategy also communicate something entirely different. War is based on the destruction of the enemy, and it is expected that casualties will be incurred in pursuit of this goal. When compared to the direct approach, the indirect strategy results in the least loss. Employing the indirect strategy does not sap the strength of the winner and waste valuable resources. In Sun Tzu's words, "The clever fighter is one who not only wins, but excels in winning with ease."[12] The practitioner of the direct strategy, in contrast, runs a bigger risk of losing and pays a heavier price in order to win. Simply put, the indirect strategy is the easiest and most economical way to win.

Another master practitioner of the indirect strategy was Napoleon Bonaparte. In fact, Napoleon studied Sun Tzu's teachings and based his tactics upon them. At the heart of Napoleon's indirect strategy are the concepts of mobility, countermoves, and speed of response. "Strategy is the art of making use of time and space. I am less concerned about the latter than the former. Space we can recover, lost time never," he said.[13]

Napoleon's battle plans consisted of several branches. Each branch was a different course of action deliberately made to influence the enemy's countermove. To execute his plan, Napoleon had to anticipate his enemy's position. For example, he would disperse his forces to cause his enemy to disperse its forces, thus creating favorable conditions for a concentrated attack at a weakened point. A master of the indirect strategy, Napoleon wrote, "The art is to extend forces without exposing them, to embrace the enemy without being disunited, to link up the moves or attacks to take to the enemy in flank without exposing one's own flank."[14]

Throughout Napoleon's reign, France was considered a rogue nation, which prompted all the European nations to band together in attempts to overthrow its leader. In 1805, Napoleon staged 50,000 of his troops in Bruun, Austria, in order to present to the opposing Russian commanders and their 80,000 troops the impression of weakness. At the same time, he sent word to the Russian tsar and the Austrian emperor (Russia's ally) of his desire for peace. These acts further instilled in the Russian commanders a belief in Napoleon's vulnerability.

As part of his plan, Napoleon secretly sent several detachments forward. Then he gave the impression that the left flank of his line was in retreat. The Russians, now fully convinced that they had a chance to destroy the French army, decided to attack. Exactly as predicted, the Russian forces set out in pursuit of the retreating French troops, who led them through unfavorable terrain to a valley where French cannons had been previously positioned in the hills above. Napoleon then swung his army around against the center of the spread-out Russian line. The Russian army, split in two and under concentrated cannon fire, was crushed. The next day the tsar and the Austrian emperor asked for peace. The Russians had fallen into Napoleon's trap. His strategy enabled his smaller army to defeat a larger one.

Nearly 140 years later, another military leader earned his place in history using the indirect strategy. General George Patton didn't mince words when he advised his commanders to "hold them by the nose and kick them in the pants."[15] In effect, he was actually describing his particular flavor of indirect strategy. General Patton also played a surprising role in one of the biggest examples of the indirect strategy in military history, Operation Overlord, the D-Day invasion of France during World War II.

By the summer of 1944, the German army was expecting an Allied invasion and had heavily fortified the English Channel coastline. The Germans believed the most likely invasion point would be Pas-de-Calais, France, where the distance between England and Europe was shortest. In order to reinforce this belief, the Allies created an imaginary invasion force headed by General Patton. False radio messages were sent, decoy troop movements were made, and inflatable tanks were set up to give the impression that a well-armed force led by Patton was being prepared for an invasion at Pas-de-Calais.

However, the biggest naval invasion in history up to that time would occur hundreds of miles to the southwest on the beaches of Normandy. Even days after the successful D-Day landing, the German high command still believed the real invasion was yet to come at Pas-de-Calais. The misdirection had worked perfectly, and a substantial portion of the Nazi army was kept in check at the wrong place. In effect, the diversion held it by the nose while it was being kicked in the pants.

THE SEVEN PRINCIPLES OF THE INDIRECT STRATEGY

Seven principles underlie the indirect strategy. The first and foremost principle is that the indirect strategy is a psychological operation ("psy-op" in military jargon) based on understanding, predicting, and influencing human nature. Psy-ops include the manipulation of information, movements, and positioning to gain a strategic battlefield advantage before and during a war. On the battlefield, the mission of psy-ops is to cause the enemy to quit by inflicting mental and emotional trauma. The goal is to elevate the enemy's combat fatigue and skepticism about winning, because a halfhearted warrior is more than halfway to losing.

The second and third principles are based upon the elimination of the "fog of war," the natural uncertainty and lack of knowledge that occur during the heat of battle. The word *war* is derived from the Frankish-German word *werra*, which means confusion, discord, or strife.[16] The second principle is that effective communications are necessary to eliminate miscues and mistakes, while the third principle is that privileged intelligence is a requirement to win a war. Only through privileged intelligence can one determine the enemy's position and find its weaknesses.

In battle, the only certainty is change. Constantly changing battle conditions require flexible tactics. Generals' success lies not only in their initial plans but in how they adapt their plans once the initial plan has become inconsequential. The fourth principle is tactical flexibility, knowing when to use the optimum maneuver—a surprise attack, calculated retreat, coordinated counterattack, or defensive position—at the appropriate time. The fifth principle acknowledges that time is the ultimate enemy. During a prolonged engagement, the relentless march of time depletes supplies, weapons, troops, and morale.

The sixth principle, that deception is at the heart of the indirect strategy, and the seventh principle, that every battle has a turning point, are intimately intertwined. The indirect strategy is based on the creation of deceptions to confuse enemies. This confusion creates a critical turning point, causing enemies to lose momentum they can never regain.

Let's review these seven principles in further detail and discuss their application to sales.

The Indirect Strategy Is Based on Psychology and Human Nature

In the third century B.C., Chinese Emperor Ch'in Shih Huang Ti ordered the building of a great wall to keep the Mongols from attacking his empire. He dictated that the wall should be five men high and six horses wide, with watchtowers posted every three hundred feet. Surprisingly, invaders overcame this seemingly impenetrable barrier three times during the first one hundred years of its existence alone. The invading armies didn't have to take long marches around it or incur huge losses trying to scale it in a massive frontal assault. All they had to do was bribe the guards who manned the gates.

The best way to win a war is not to have to fight it at all. Sun Tzu said, "To fight and conquer all your battles is not supreme excellence; supreme excellence consists of breaking the enemy's resistance without fighting."[17] If you win the psychological war with a customer, you will have defeated your enemy before the battle has even begun. If your competitors believe you to be in a position of such strength, they will make at best a halfhearted effort. More importantly, they will be constantly off balance, lacking the intestinal fortitude to execute their plans, and they will be more likely to make a fatal faux pas during the sales cycle.

In sales, we ideally want to place our competitors at a psychological disadvantage, even before the battle begins. We want to instill a preconceived notion of our advantages in both the competitors' and the customer's minds. The advertisements, web sites, and other marketing messages our company broadcasts to the marketplace are like prestrike air cover prior to the ground assault by salespeople in the field.

However, based on my personal experience, the only dependable air cover is that carried out by the salespeople themselves. They must target an account and make it aware of their company's products well in advance of a possible sales opportunity. Fortunately, it has never been easier to stay in touch with prospective customers. Internet technology provides the ability to send e-mails and electronic newsletters and to conduct webinars with prospects well in advance of a face-to-face meeting.

Gaining a psychological advantage with customers is our first goal. This requires understanding customers' deep-seated desires, motivations, fears, and frustrations. Napoleon called these "their virtues, their vices, their heroism, their perverseness" and whether "they possess and exercise all that is good, and all that is bad."[18]

A study of the great wars confirms that winning can occur only when one has the psychological advantage. Germany surrendered in World War I when its demoralized citizens lost the will to fight. Similarly, the United States sought an exit strategy in Vietnam when the American psyche turned against the war. Take a moment to think about the last three deals you won. What was your psychological advantage?

Communication Is the Cornerstone of the Indirect Strategy

On June 25, 1876, General George Armstrong Custer died on the plains of Montana in the battle of Little Big Horn. Almost every Western history buff knows that the 210 soldiers of the Seventh Cavalry under his command that day were wiped out. However, the circumstances leading up to the battle are relatively unknown.

On the morning of June 25, the 676 soldiers of the Seventh Cavalry separated into three regiments in preparation for an attack on an Indian village of some 8,000 men, women, and children. The attack was planned based on the indirect strategy according to the *U.S. Army Cavalry Tactics and Regulations Manual*, which stated, "If possible, at the moment of a charge, assail your enemy in the flank when the enemy is engaged in the front."[19] Custer's regiment would advance upon Little Big Horn in the front, while the other regiments, headed by Major Marcus Reno and Captain Frederick Benteen, would move into positions parallel to the village and launch a coordinated attack on the flanks.

After being spotted by Indian scouts, Custer feared that the Indians would slip away as they had done in the past. Because he lacked patience and was in search of fame, he disobeyed orders and decided to launch a direct assault on the village. However, prior to making his attack, he sent at least two messages to Reno and Benteen ordering them to advance at once. While historians still debate why they did not carry out those orders, there is no debate about Custer's destruction. Within 50 minutes of the start of the attack, all of Custer's soldiers had been killed, stripped, scalped, and mutilated—a violent end to an imprudent direct attack.

"The secret of war lies in the communications," according to Napoleon.[20] Maintaining command, control, and coordination of fighting forces over great distances requires constant communication. As a result, armies had to create their own languages to concisely convey messages with exact accuracy in the shortest possible time. For example, a World War II U.S. army radioman might have said, "Lemon Red 6 Able, this is Lagoon White 3," which meant "Battalion operations officer, Second Battalion, 115th Infantry regiment is calling for the radio operator for the commander, First Battalion, 116th Infantry regiment."[21]

Similarly, every industry today has its own language to ensure accurate and effective communication. For example, a semiconductor salesperson might tell a design engineer at a wireless phone company that his "1,575.42-megahertz SAW filter has a usable bandwidth of 2.4 megahertz." A computer salesperson might describe his server to an information technology professional as "four 3.3-gigahertz 64-bit processors, 40-gigabyte memory, and 360-gigabyte hard drive storage." These are just two of the different types of languages a customer speaks that must be analyzed, interpreted, and understood.

War, like sales, entails three types of communication: orders that deliver instructions, messages that motivate or persuade, and messages that transmit intelligence. Of these three types of communication, none is more important to both the battlefield commander and the salesperson than intelligence, secret information about enemies.

The Indirect Strategy Requires Privileged Intelligence

Can you imagine being forewarned about every move your competitors were going to make before they made them? That's the advantage the Allies had during World War II. The German military used the Enigma cipher machine to encrypt its communications. The German army, navy, and air force all encoded their messages, believing their secrecy was maintained. However, one of the war's best-kept secrets was that British code breakers had cracked the Enigma code and were able to decipher every communication.

Intelligence played an equally important role in the Pacific theater. The war effort against Japan had gone badly since the attack on Pearl Harbor. The Japanese controlled the southwest Pacific and Southeast Asia. The Allies did not know where the Japanese would invade next: Australia, New Zealand, Hawaii, or even the mainland United States.

Most of the traditional sources of wartime intelligence, such as captured documents, flight reconnaissance, and prisoner interrogations, were not available in the early stages of the war. The only source of intelligence was radio communications. U.S. naval intelligence broke the Japanese code and established radio intercept monitoring stations in Hawaii, the Philippines, Guam, and Bainbridge Island, Washington. However, by March 1942, the Philippines and Guam monitoring stations were lost to the Japanese advance.

In May 1942, thousands of messages had been deciphered about a huge Japanese armada that was heading toward Midway Island. Naval intelligence officers had pieced together the essentials of the Japanese operation. They knew the names of the ships and that almost the entire Japanese fleet would attack on June 4 at Midway Island. In response, the U.S. Navy marshaled its ships and prepared for the imminent assault.

The Battle of Midway was a decisive American victory and the turning point of the Pacific war. After the three days of fighting, the Japanese had lost four carriers and hundreds of irreplaceable fighter pilots. The battle stopped the expansion of the Japanese Empire, which would be on the defensive for the remainder of the war. Fleet commander Admiral Chester Nimitz said after the battle, "Had we lacked early information of the Japanese movement, and had we been caught with Carrier Task Forces dispersed, possibly as far away as the Coral Sea, the Battle of Midway would have ended far differently."[22]

While Admiral Nimitz relied mainly on intercepted communications to gather privileged intelligence, a salesperson must rely almost exclusively on the use of spies. These spies are members of the selection team and other company employees. Sometimes, enemy secrets come from other valuable sources of information, such as consultants or business partners.

"Knowledge of the enemy's position can only be obtained from other men. Hence, the use of spies," Sun Tzu said.[23] These words are as true today as they were two and a half thousand years ago. In order to win any deal, you need proprietary information that only a spy can provide. Without a spy, you never know how well you are positioned in an account or what the enemy's next move will be, and you are susceptible to surprises throughout the sales cycle.

The Indirect Strategy Is Flexible, Employing Attacks, Retreats, and Defensive Fighting Based on Circumstances

The situation was grim when George Washington solemnly addressed the Continental Congress about the fight for independence in 1776. Outnumbered and ill-equipped, the nature of the colonies' circumstances mandated that they adopt an indirect strategy to win. Washington stressed that the only way the Continental Army could defeat the British was to fight defensively: "On our side, the war should be defensive . . . we are now in a dangerous position. Declining an engagement to fight may throw discouragement over the minds of many, but when the fate of America may be at stake, we should continue the war as long as possible."[24]

The Continental Army would have to wage a war of attrition rather than challenge a superior foe to a conventional fight. In essence, the defensive strategy would be used in an offensive way. In the words of the famous Prussian general Helmuth von Moltke, "A clever military leader will succeed in many cases in choosing defensive positions of such an offensive nature from the strategic point of view that the enemy is compelled to attack us in them."[25]

The fourth principle of the indirect strategy is that attacking, retreating, and fighting defensively are all necessary, depending on the nature of the enemy. The concept of "tactical flexibility" was best described by Sun Tzu when he said, "If the enemy is in superior strength, avoid him. If your opponent is of choleric temper, seek to irritate him. Pretend to be weak, that he may grow arrogant. If he is taking his ease, give him no rest. If his forces are united, separate them. Attack him where he is unprepared, appear where you are not expected."[26]

The essence of Napoleonic warfare was to upset the enemy's balance. Military historians debate the "one point" of attack Napoleon referred to when he said, "The principles of war are the same as those of a siege. Fire must be concentrated at one point, and as soon as the breach is made, the equilibrium is broken and the rest is nothing."[27] Did he mean attack the enemy at its strongest point and once this strategic position is taken the remaining defensive positions will fall, or did he mean attack the enemy at its weakest spot in order to breach its line of defense? Historical analysis of Napoleon's battles shows he actually meant both. At times, Napoleon would focus his efforts on the enemy's strength and at other times on its weakness. Moreover, it was a dynamic strategy that changed with the lay of the land and nature of the enemy.

Every battle recorded throughout history has been unique. Battles have been fought by different armies with different plans, weapons, and troop concentrations upon different terrain in different weather and at different times of day. Similarly, every deal a salesperson works on is unique. Each deal involves different people with unique personalities, one-of-a-kind customer requirements and selection processes, and extraordinary decision-making politics. Therefore, the strategy and tactical plans to win each account should be unique as well. The salesperson who employs the same tactics for every account is making a mistake. In the words of Patton, your goal is to "make your plans to fit the circumstances, not the other way around."[28]

Salespeople must motivate customers to believe in them and at the same time lure enemies (competitors) to attack them under unfavorable circumstances. Sometimes a calculated withdrawal, dropping an account, is absolutely necessary to protect precious resources: time, manpower, and mental and emotional energy. However, the sales management at many companies won't let salespeople drop deals. Even though a salesperson believes the chance of winning is zero, these companies insist that the deal be worked until the conclusion, when the customer makes a public announcement of the vendor who won. In some cases, the political bureaucracy of a sales organization prevents deals from being dropped. Removing a deal from the forecast is virtually impossible because of the deal's exposure to senior sales management. This "false forecasting" of an impossible deal benefits no one: salespeople, management, or the company as a whole.

The Indirect Strategy Employs Rapid Dominance to Defeat the Ultimate Enemy—Time

On March 20, 2003, Operation Iraqi Freedom's "shock and awe" campaign began with precision strikes of Tomahawk missiles and laser-guided bombs intended to destroy high-value military targets in Iraq and eliminate high-level political officials, including Saddam Hussein. Over the next three weeks, the world watched on live television the destruction of the Iraqi army and the capture of

Baghdad in an astounding display of weaponry and speed of attack. By every military standard—coalition losses, civilian casualties, and the extreme Iraqi military losses—the shock and awe campaign was a complete success. This was due in large part to the fact that the entire operation was based on the interdependence between indirect strategy and the element of time.

After the city of Baghdad was surrounded, the U.S. Army's Third Infantry sent a tank column storming through the streets in what is called a "thunder run." The goal of the surprise sortie was to test Iraqi defensive positions, but it was also a demonstration of military prowess aimed at preventing street-to-street fighting. It was theorized that a thundering column of tanks rolling through the city would convince the Iraqi military defenders, leaders, and any citizen militia that resistance would be futile.

One day after the first thunder run, the Third Infantry made another one. Resistance was so light that the tanks kept going and drove straight into Saddam Hussein's palace, where the soldiers established a base. The capital had been conquered with barely a fight. As television crews beamed the event around the world, it was obvious to all concerned that the conventional fighting was over. The speed at which the invaders had driven over the borders and into downtown Baghdad had caused the regime and its military forces to collapse.

The shock and awe campaign of the Iraq war was based on the military doctrine of rapid dominance originated by Harlan Ullman and James Wade. Ullman's book, *Shock and Awe: Achieving Rapid Dominance*, defines rapid dominance as follows: " 'Rapid' means the ability to move quickly before an adversary can react. This notion of rapidity applies throughout the spectrum of combat from pre-conflict deployment to all stages of battle and conflict resolution. 'Dominance' means the ability to affect and dominate an adversary's will both physically and psychologically. Physical dominance includes the ability to destroy, disarm, disrupt, neutralize, and render impotent."[29]

The military leader breaks down time into several elements: preparation time, exposure time, and the moment of attack. Patton wrote in his letters of instruction to his commanders, "Take plenty of time to set up an attack. A pint of sweat will save a gallon of blood!" and, once an attack has begun, "Inflict the maximum amount of wounds, death, and destruction in the minimum time. Casualties vary directly to the amount of time you are exposed to effective fire. Rapidity of attack shortens the time of exposure."[30]

Another special moment, the moment to attack, is more important than all others. Recognizing and acting at that moment is key. Action is hesitation's enemy. Among military leaders there is an adage that a 70 percent solution acted on immediately is always better than a perfect solution acted on later. A general considers time a real enemy.

Time is a salesperson's enemy because time is finite. On average, there are 30 days in a month and 90 days in a quarter. Time is the governor that determines how many deals can be worked and where effort should be focused. The relentless march of time creates artificial deadlines by which deals must be won. Time is a precious resource that must be conserved, respected, and, above all, used to one's advantage. As Sun Tzu commented, "Rapidity is the essence of war; take advantage of the enemy's unreadiness, make your way by unexpected routes, and attack unguarded spots."[31] To a military man, the old saying "Time is money" is actually wrong. Time is much more valuable than money. It is actually life and the difference between the living and the dead.

Deception Is at the Heart of the Indirect Strategy

Based on its experiences with trench warfare in World War I, the French government built seemingly impenetrable fortifications on its German border between 1929 and 1940. This great 400-mile network of bunkers, tunnels, and ditches was named the Maginot

Line after the beloved war hero André Maginot. The Maginot Line provided France with a false sense of security that a German attack would be held in check far away from the cities. After all, the trenches of World War I had held the Kaiser's army at bay for four years.

When the German army began its western offensive in May 1940, it took great care to avoid a direct assault on the Maginot Line. Instead, the Germans chose to use an indirect strategy to lure the Allies out from behind their defenses. The bait they used was a fraction of their army sent to attack Holland and Belgium. In response, the French command pushed forward French and British troops in a massive counterattack against the decoy army. Unfortunately, the French command didn't realize the real German attack would occur through the Ardennes Forest, which it had left lightly defended. Within 12 days of the deceptive attack, the German army had overrun France, the British forces were expelled from Europe, and the French government capitulated.

"All warfare is based upon deception," Sun Tzu said. His advice about deceiving the enemy could also be applied to salespeople who must deceive the competition: "When able to attack, we must seem unable; when using our forces, we must seem inactive; when we are near, we must make the enemy believe we are far away; when far away, we must make him believe we are near." Salespeople must be experts at creating deceptions so that "the opposition believes you are weak when you are strong."[32]

Salespeople expect deception from competitors. However, the most damaging deceptions actually come from customers. Customers will say what they don't mean and mean what they don't say. Salespeople are on a mission to learn the ultimate truth, "Will I win the deal?" Meanwhile, whether inadvertently or on purpose, customers will lie. Napoleon summed up the situation well when he said, "Flatterers and men of learning do not accord well with each other."[33]

The Indirect Strategy Seeks to Create a Turning Point or Moment That Determines the Winner and Loser

In 1944, General Vo Nguyen Giap led a small attack force against a strategic French outpost in Indochina. He chose Christmas Eve to launch the surprise attack and won a stunning victory. Nearly 25 years later, General Giap would plan another daring attack against American and South Vietnamese forces in Vietnam. The attack would occur on the eve of the most important Vietnamese holiday, the lunar new year festival of Tet Nguyen Dan.

The Tet offensive was the coordinated attack on more than 30 South Vietnamese cities on January 30, 1968, by North Vietnamese forces. From a military standpoint, the attackers were defeated; nearly 60,000 North Vietnamese troops were killed compared to the 4,000 U.S. troops who lost their lives.[34] However, the goal of Giap's attack was more than military targets; it was political defeat. By this standard, the attack was a complete victory and the turning point of the war.

The Tet offensive was a media disaster for President Lyndon Johnson. Only days before, U.S. military leaders had painted an optimistic picture of the Vietnam War. Now television viewers in the United States were watching bloody battles on the streets of Saigon and seeing the U.S. embassy under attack. Graphic newspaper photos and television news footage, like the famous pistol-to-the-head execution of a Vietcong guerrilla, captured the violent nature of war. Within weeks, the Tet offensive swayed the American public against the war. Less than a year later, a new president was elected who promised to bring peace and honor to Vietnam.

Like war, every deal has a critical moment, or turning point, that determines the winner and the loser. In some cases, the turning point is easy to spot. For example, a salesperson presenting his solution may encounter a deal-breaking objection that he is unable to overcome. Even though the customer remains cordial for the rest of the meeting, a turning point has occurred and the deal is lost. In most cases, the turning point occurs when the salesperson isn't present. In casual hallway conversations or internal e-mails, selection team members share opinions that influence a vendor's future.

Napoleon described the nature of the turning point when he said, "Sometimes a single battle decides everything and sometimes, too, the slightest circumstance decides the issue of a battle. There is a moment in every battle at which the least manoeuvre is decisive and gives superiority, as one drop of water causes overflow."[35]

All seven principles of the indirect strategy share a common foundation: they are based on innovation, creativity, and boldness. Around 1200 B.C. the Greeks devised a daring plan to conquer Troy. After attacking the city without success, they built a large wooden horse and sailed away. At night, after the Trojans had moved the horse within the city walls, Greek soldiers emerged from within the horse and opened the city gates for their comrades. It was their out-of-the-box thinking that enabled the Greeks to win the war. An old military saying is that blunders can be forgiven, but a lack of boldness cannot. Or in the words of Patton, "If everyone is thinking alike, someone isn't thinking."[36]

The seven principles of indirect strategy are interdependent and should always occur together. For example, the military execution of the shock and awe campaign in the Iraq war was preceded by a psychological shock and awe campaign aimed at breaking the Iraqi army's will to fight. Prior to the attack, U.S. military leaders briefed the news agencies about the six hundred laser-guided missiles that would be launched in the first two days of the invasion, twice as many as during the entire 1991 Gulf War. They also explained how six thousand satellite guidance kits had been fitted on "dumb bombs" to turn them into "smart bombs." The news agencies in turn quoted Pentagon officials about the magnitude of the offensive: "The sheer size of this has never been seen before, never been contemplated before. There will not be a safe place in Baghdad."[37] Clearly, the attack on the Iraqi psyche was another coordinated attack on the enemy. "Battles are won by frightening the enemy," according to Patton.[38]

Frightening the enemy is an important concept in business as well. Most companies don't realize that one of marketing's most important objectives is to scare the competition. While a company's advertising, its press announcements, and the depth and breadth of its web site are directed at customers, they serve another very important purpose: they frighten the competition's salespeople in the field.

THE INDIRECT STRATEGY IN SALES

During my 20-year sales career, I intuitively practiced the indirect strategy to win over customers. Moreover, the hundreds of Heavy Hitters (truly great salespeople) whom I worked with, managed, and interviewed over the years were also expert practitioners. Whereas any salesperson can lecture a customer on product benefits or dispute a competitor's accusations, Heavy Hitters sabotage competitors using the indirect strategy.

Thinking back about it now, one of my main duties as a vice president of sales was to mentor less-experienced salespeople on the virtues of the indirect attack over the direct attack. It seems that junior salespeople are much more eager to present, pressure, and confront rather than persuade. Most interestingly, over the course of the past three years, I have had the privilege of interviewing several hundred Heavy Hitter salespeople across all types of industries. While their selling styles vary greatly, they all share one similar characteristic: each has mastered the indirect approach to sales.

As salespeople, our world is structured on a value system that is intimately tied to the production of a single revenue number. This number is how the rest of our world measures our contribution, and it is also how we tend to judge our own worth. The pressure that is inherent in sales constantly prompts salespeople to use the direct approach.

As a result, we focus the process of selling on a series of logical steps. A simple example of these steps might be to initially qualify the account, present our solution, create a call to action, and ask for the business. We mistakenly believe this straight-line approach to sales is the most effective way to win. Another oversight is that we can mistakenly assume our competition will adhere to the same steps. However, the history of war has proved time and time again that the quickest way to win is not always the most obvious. As Liddell Hart said, "The longest way round is often the shortest way home."[39] The indirect strategy is not a straight-line approach to sales.

Many salespeople who are familiar with the term *flanking* mistakenly equate it to the indirect strategy. Flanking is a battle-field movement that consists of changing one's position to gain an advantage. For example, salespeople may change the topic of conversation to a strong point about their product in order to avoid a discussion about a deficiency. While the flanking tactic may be part of the indirect strategy, it is not the strategy itself.

CLOSING THOUGHTS

All sales is war. It is an intense, high-stakes, very personal battle between two individuals or two groups of people: you and your main competition. The victor will savor the spoils of winning while the loser experiences humiliation and sometimes much worse. The indirect strategy has been proven throughout history to be the most successful approach to winning wars.

In the business world, the indirect strategy can also be used to bring products to market and improve market share at the expense of your archenemy. At the account executive level, the indirect strategy will enable you to win more deals. Given the nature of to-day's customers, the indirect strategy is the key to winning our daily sales battles. Regardless of whether they are used to drive a companywide initiative or close an individual deal, the seven underlying principles of the indirect strategy ensure a successful operation. In the next chapter, we examine the tactics associated with each of these principles.

Let's end this chapter with another look at the Civil War in light of the indirect strategy. While the Battle of Gettysburg is remembered as the war's turning point, the Union victory was in fact due to a switch in strategies from direct to indirect. The indirect strategy was employed by Generals William Tecumseh Sherman and Ulysses S. Grant hundreds of miles away from Gettysburg. General Sherman's famous march to the sea was an entirely defensive attack designed to wreak havoc behind enemy lines. The goal was not to engage the enemy directly but to scorch the earth upon which the enemy depended.

After several unsuccessful direct attempts to take the city of Vicksburg, Mississippi, General Grant had learned an important lesson. A by-product of the attacks, the continuous hammering upon the Confederate Army and weakening of its resolve to fight, was equally important to the military goal of capturing the city. When Grant later became supreme commander of all Union forces, he directed his troops to harass the enemy, to never let the enemy rest and regroup, and to keep moving regardless of a battle's outcome. Winning the psychological war became just as important as winning the contest on the battlefield.

The Confederate leaders initially did not believe the Union populace would have the resolve to fight a long war. They planned to fight a protracted war and make the endeavor as costly as possible. They thought time was on their side. However, because of Sherman's and Grant's use of the indirect strategy, the passage of time became an ally of the Union. In turn, the Confederates were forced to engage in a decisive battle that they hoped would end the war. It was the Union's indirect strategy that compelled Lee to attack at Gettysburg. In the prophetic words of Sun Tzu, "The clever combatant imposes his will on the enemy, but does not allow the enemy's will to be imposed on him."[40]

Your competitors seek to destroy you. They have educated themselves about your products and sales tactics, and they're focused on defeating you more than ever. Fortunately, they usually believe in the use of brute force and think the best way to defeat you is by direct frontal attack. In reality, an indirect strategy of winning over the hearts and minds of customers carries the day.

CHAPTER 2

Battlefield Tactics

May God have mercy upon my enemies, because I won't.
—GENERAL GEORGE S. PATTON
War as I Knew It

On June 5, 1944, General George Patton addressed his Third
Army as it prepared for the next day's invasion of Europe. For
many soldiers in the unit, this would be their first taste of battle,
and Patton knew they felt equal amounts of apprehension and
angst. Dressed in full uniform, wearing a shiny silver helmet and
his favorite ivory-handled Colt pistol at his side, Patton delivered a
speech that was part pep rally and part farewell address to calm the
soldiers' jittery nerves.

That famous speech would later be recreated at the beginning
of the 1970 motion picture *Patton*. However, the movie did not include what I consider the most relevant part of the speech for those
of us in sales. Patton's actual words help explain the innate competition inside each of us and its despised counterpart, fear. The passage that follows consists of his unedited words, curses and all.
After all, it was "Blood and Guts" Patton who once said, "You can't
run an army without profanity; and it has to be eloquent profanity.
An army without profanity couldn't fight its way out of a piss-
soaked paper bag."[1]

> Men, this stuff that some sources sling around about Amer-
> ica wanting out of this war, not wanting to fight, is a crock
> of bullshit. Americans love to fight, traditionally. All real

Americans love the sting and clash of battle. You are here today for three reasons. First, because you are here to defend your homes and your loved ones. Second, you are here for your own self-respect, because you would not want to be anywhere else. Third, you are here because you are real men and all real men like to fight. When you, here, everyone of you, were kids, you all admired the champion marble player, the fastest runner, the toughest boxer, the big league ballplayers, and the All-American football players. Americans love a winner. Americans will not tolerate a loser. Americans despise cowards. Americans play to win all of the time. I wouldn't give a hoot in hell for a man who lost and laughed.

Death must not be feared. Death, in time, comes to all men. Yes, every man is scared in his first battle. If he says he's not, he's a liar. . . . The real hero is the man who fights even though he is scared. . . . A real man will never let his fear of death overpower his honor, his sense of duty to his country, and his innate manhood. Battle is the most magnificent competition in which a human being can indulge.[2]

Sales, too, is a magnificent competition that continually requires you to face your fears. Sales and soldiering are both occupations where survival and success are based on causing the opponent's demise. Although it is not fought with deadly weapons, sales is a one-on-one fight nonetheless. It's a war fought with words.

Sales is unlike most other professions. While doctors save lives, teachers build lives, and police officers protect lives, salespeople are on a mission to actually destroy the lives of their competitors. Salespeople are verbal warriors who seek to crush their enemies emotionally and psychologically. As salespeople, we want our competitors to question whether they are working for the right company, to lose faith in their sales skills, and even to second-guess themselves about whether they belong in this profession at all. Our goal is to annihilate the competition. Customers are the weapons we use to accomplish this mission.

Since customers do not provide us the opportunity for a face-to-face fight, we don't get the chance to confront our enemies in person. Rather, our enemies' destruction is based on having the customer choose us over them. Rejection is a real killer. It obliterates faith, dreams, and careers. Rejection can stamp out a salesperson's soul just as a bullet can snuff out the life of an infantryman.

Defeating the enemy and winning the war is based on the indirect strategy of winning over customers. The magnificence of our battle is in winning the trust, respect, and friendship of another human being, thereby causing our adversaries' demise. The victor builds the strongest customer relationship, manages the selection process better, and outmaneuvers his enemies over the customer's political landscape (the various decision makers involved in the selection process). The champion outsmarts, outhustles, and outwits the losers.

Defeating the enemy does not require you to be the most knowledgeable salesperson, have the most technically proficient product, or be the best debater. Think back for a moment to the 2004 U.S. presidential election. Senator John Kerry was a skilled debater who won every presidential campaign debate, according to the experts. However, George W. Bush won the election, and exit polls proved it wasn't because more people agreed with his policies. Bush won because he was able to connect with voters better than Kerry was. Bush's grand strategy was based on the use of the indirect strategy. (We'll learn much more about this in Chapter 5.)

GRAND STRATEGY, BATTLES, AND BATTLEFIELD MANEUVERS

All wars can be broken down into three elements: grand strategy, battles, and battlefield maneuvers. The grand strategy is the overall approach to how the war will be won. In sales, the grand strategy should always be based on an indirect approach to influence the people, selection process, and politics of the customer's decision making. The grand strategy is accomplished by executing a series of battles (sales calls, presentations, demonstrations, and so on), each of which may be based on an indirect or direct approach, depending on the circumstances.

Finally, the smallest element of war consists of battlefield maneuvers. Battlefield maneuvers (such as phone calls, letters, and e-mails) are specific actions intended to move a salesperson to the next battle. Although they are typically small steps, they can have a great impact on the deal. For example, let's say a customer is looking at a competitor's product and hesitates to meet with you. A battlefield maneuver might be to e-mail the customer an industry article that rates your product better than the competitor's. After reading the article, the customer may decide to let you present your solution. The idea is that you have to maneuver into position to fight the first battle.

Battlefield maneuvers prevent you from standing still, getting stuck at a certain stage in the sales cycle, or being pinned down by an opponent's tactics. These maneuvers are usually based on a direct approach. Figure 2.1 illustrates the interrelationships between grand strategy, battles, and battlefield maneuvers.

The sales cycle is a sequence of battles or action points, such as sales calls, presentations, demonstrations, surveys, and site visits. However, each party participating in these battles has different goals. Your competitors are trying to eliminate you from the next battle. Meanwhile, you are a suitor, trying to court a customer into forming a long-term relationship, akin to a marriage. You try to ac-

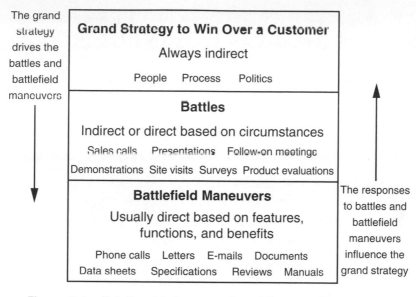

The grand strategy drives the battles and battlefield maneuvers

Grand Strategy to Win Over a Customer

Always indirect

People   Process   Politics

Battles

Indirect or direct based on circumstances

Sales calls   Presentations   Follow-on meetings

Demonstrations   Site visits   Surveys   Product evaluations

Battlefield Maneuvers

Usually direct based on features, functions, and benefits

Phone calls   Letters   E-mails   Documents

Data sheets   Specifications   Reviews   Manuals

The responses to battles and battlefield maneuvers influence the grand strategy

Figure 2.1   Relationship between Grand Strategy, Battles, and Battlefield Maneuvers

complish this by scheduling battles to explain your product's features and benefits and the merits of your company. These events give you opportunities to befriend and win over the customer.

Customers have a different set of goals. Relationships are expensive and involve investments of valuable time and money. Customers have to spend time to determine whether a product's characteristics are as they have been represented. They have to spend time evaluating other suitors to determine whether they are picking the best possible partner. They have to spend time learning to use the new products they select, implementing them, and most likely, fixing product problems. In addition, customers have to acquire the solution and pay ongoing fees for support. They want to make sure they are selecting the best partner and have found their "soul mate." Your battlefield maneuvers may include facts and other proof points that put the customer's mind at ease and move you to the next battle, the next step in the sales cycle.

During a long sales cycle of several months or more, it's easy to focus on individual battles and lose sight of winning the war. The sales cycle is reduced to a series of battles without an overriding grand strategy. We become fixated on the next battle, proceeding from the initial call to the sales presentation, from the presentation to the demonstration, and from the demonstration to the product evaluation. Usually, the salesperson who experiences an eleventh-hour defeat fought in this battle du jour (battle of the day) manner without a grand strategy. The moment you work on an account without a grand strategy, you relinquish account control. Worse yet is when the details of the battles—where, when, and how they will be fought—are out of your control because they are determined exclusively by the customer or even a competitor.

Meanwhile, competitors are trying to outdo and sabotage you with their own battlefield maneuvers. For example, they'll provide the customer with believable information that contradicts yours. Therefore, the sales cycle naturally disintegrates into a "he said—she said" type of quarrel. This leaves the customer not only confused but sometimes in "analysis paralysis" due to receiving too much contradictory information, which sets the stage for the dreaded no decision. If you find yourself in an account bickering with a competitor, take a step back and ask yourself these three questions:

1. What is my grand strategy? Did I take time to create one in the first place?

2. Am I confusing battlefield maneuvers or my involvement in a sequence of battles with a grand strategy?

3. Is the customer or competition dictating when, how, and where the battles will be fought?

Battlefield maneuvers are calculated actions intended to influence battles. Sometimes the smallest maneuver can determine the outcome of an entire war. An example of a battlefield maneuver that had great influence is the development of the Napoleonic cannon. The armies of the time marched into battle in closely arranged lines to consolidate and synchronize their musket fire. However, instead of loading his cannons with a single large cannonball, Napoleon loaded them with grape-sized shot. The grapeshot was much more effective than single-shot cannons since it had a wider kill zone. This single maneuver changed Napoleon's grand strategy of waging war.

The grapeshot salespeople use is usually provided by the marketing department. However, the marketing departments at most companies generally don't truly understand what salespeople do. To those departments, selling is a series of steps that prospects are guided through. These steps are based on the logic of purchasing a product, and the marketing team's job is to provide the tools to move prospects to the next step. Meanwhile, salespeople must work with the unpredictable part of the process: people. Their job is to formulate an account strategy based on the people they are trying to sell to.

Marketing departments almost always believe in using the direct strategy exclusively. They mistakenly think that customers' decision-making processes are completely unbiased and purely rational. As a result, they crank out data sheets, white papers, press releases, return on investment studies, and other forms of company propaganda. They will call their companies the "world leader," "industry leader," or "global provider." They will say their products are "innovative," "state-of-the-art," and "easy to use." They will explain how their products increase revenues, cut costs, and improve customer satisfaction.

While marketing departments believe these are grand strategies, in reality they are battlefield maneuvers. They are volleys of information intended to persuade the customer to invite the salespeople to the next battle. However, they are not as effective as grapeshot from Napoleon's cannons. Usually, these marketing claims fall on deaf ears because they are neutralized by the battlefield maneuvers of competitors. However, marketers continue to have a mistaken view of the strength of these claims and how they will have a positive impact on a salesperson's position in the account.

CHARTING YOUR POSITION

Not until the sixteenth century did military mapmaking as we know it come into existence in Europe. Barbarian armies, accustomed to ransacking towns and cities at will, increasingly encountered sophisticated fortifications. To break into these walled fortresses, they developed new types of weapons and artillery. In response, the cities developed more sophisticated defense schemes with interlocking artillery fire covering every possible angle of attack. Therefore, precise cartographic information on the exact placement of guns was needed by both the defender and the attacker.

By the eighteenth century, the coordination of foot soldiers, cavalry, and artillery required detailed battle plans that showed topographic features, buildings, and enemy emplacements. Napoleon placed vital importance on the preciseness of his battle maps. He enlarged the French army's cartographic branch and established mapmaking standards so his maps could be universally understood by his troops. His detailed maps of potential military campaigns were drawn up well in advance of each offensive and updated afterward. When he invaded Egypt in 1798, he brought with him over one hundred scientists, geographers, and mapmakers, who created the first detailed maps of the country.

All battlefield commanders need location-based information—the coordinates of their current location and the enemies' locations. With that, they can create a map that points the way to reaching their objective. Salespeople need the same type of information.

They need to chart their own position in an account and the positions of enemy competitors. Finally, they need a road map that shows them how to win.

In every account, salespeople will find themselves in one of five distinct positions, depending on the amount of information they have acquired and the level of rapport they have developed with the prospective customer. These positions are fortress, reconnaissance, escalade, coup de main, and retreat. Figure 2.2 shows all of these positions.

This diagram can help you determine your bearings in an account. The vertical axis indicates the amount of rapport you have with a customer. For example, a brand-new account would have low or no rapport. A high-rapport account would be one in which you have personal friendships with members of the customer's

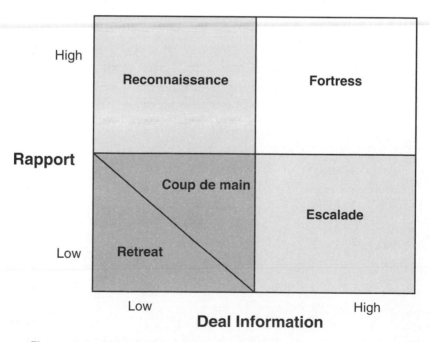

Figure 2.2 Your Position in an Account

selection team. The horizontal axis indicates the amount of truthful information being shared by the customer. This is your assessment of the quantity and quality of the information you are uncovering. It also includes any unique privileged information you are receiving that others aren't.

Your position correlates to your competitiveness in the account. If you are in the lead, you are inside the security of the fortress. In the position of reconnaissance, you have rapport, or relationships, but not enough information about the deal. Conversely, in the escalade position, you have information but not relationships. In coup de main, you are behind in the account and lack relationships and information. When you have little chance of winning, you are in retreat.

Fortress

"The fate of a nation may sometimes depend upon the position of a fortress," wrote Napoleon Bonaparte.[3] In sales, the ultimate winner is the salesperson who is inside the fortress at the end of a deal. In the fortress, you have established rapport and are receiving proprietary information that the other vendors aren't. Only one salesperson can be in the fortress at any given time. All the others are attacking from outside the walls. Sometimes a salesperson can stay inside the fortress from the beginning to the end of the sales cycle. Other times, the focused attack of all the other vendors will weaken the salesperson's position, letting someone else overtake the fortress.

Inside the fortress, an interesting paradigm shift occurs in the vendor-customer relationship. The customer begins working with the vendor as a long-term partner while they are still in the sales cycle. For example, when problems arise about the functionality of the product, the customer works with the vendor to find an acceptable solution. This shift, from being treated like one of the vendors to becoming part of the customer's team, is very noticeable. If you are the salesperson in the fortress at this point, you have won the deal and should update your forecast accordingly.

Reconnaissance

The term *reconnaissance* was derived from the French word *reconnoître,* which literally meant "to recognize."[4] Reconnaissance is the act of observing the enemy—its strength, position, and movements—in order to gain information for military purposes.

In the position of reconnaissance, you have established rapport but have a low level of information about the customer's requirements or a high level of uncertainty about whether the deal will happen. For example, you may have painstakingly developed relationships within the accounts payable group of the finance department of a Fortune 100 company. However, because of the finance department's immensity and bureaucracy, the accounts payable members are unsure of the direction and approval of their project. Therefore, even though rapport is high and the accounts payable group has identified specific business needs, the knowledge of whether a deal will be closed is lacking.

Escalade

Attacking a fortress was deadly business in medieval times, and the quickest way to take a castle, by escalade, was also the deadliest. Attackers would escalade or scale the walls using ladders. The success of the escalade was determined by speed and numbers. The ladders had to be set up quickly and in such great quantity that the defenders couldn't repulse them all.

Usually, the goal of an escalade was to infiltrate the fortress so that the main gate could be opened, thus allowing the attacking forces inside. To impede an escalade, archers were stationed on top of the walls, water-filled moats surrounded the castle, and the walls had specially constructed openings from which defenders could drop boiling oil or molten lead on attackers.

In sales, escalade techniques are based on using information to infiltrate the fortress position and to establish trusting relationships. The information could be your knowledge of the customer's industry, information about the customer's archrival, facts about the vendor in the fortress, or even unflattering details about how the selection process is occurring (for example, telling the customer selection committee leader that certain selection team members are ignoring important criteria).

A friend of mine gave me a great example of an escalade tactic. He had been trying to sell to an automobile parts manufacturer without success. The customer simply wasn't interested in meeting him and didn't want to hear about his company. However, one of my friend's other customers was General Motors, and when he offered to take the parts manufacturer to General Motors and introduce him to the executives there, he received an enthusiastic response. A few months later my friend closed his first $500,000 order with the previously unreceptive customer.

The nature of information is such that its shelf life gets shorter as the deal progresses. A salesperson must use information early in the sales cycle in order to quickly establish rapport. Without rapport, the likelihood of winning the deal decreases as the sales cycle progresses.

The amount of information salespeople receive from customers will vary. For example, the evaluation criteria could be extremely well documented. A request for proposal (RFP) may be three hundred pages long, with descriptive narrations about the customer's environment and very detailed questions about the vendor. However, this is only the external aspect of product selection. The internal, political part of product selection isn't publicly revealed. Establishing rapport is the only way to learn the true inner workings of a customer's selection process.

Coup de Main and Retreat

The bottom left-hand quadrant is where the salesperson has little information about the deal and little rapport with the customer. At the beginning of every new sales cycle, salespeople find them selves in this unenviable position. Their immediate priorities are to collect information and start the process of developing relationships in the hope of moving into the position of escalade or reconnaissance. Their ultimate goal is to be positioned inside the fortress.

Time is a salesperson's ultimate enemy. As the days and weeks slip by and no discernible movement toward the fortress quadrant takes place, the salesperson's anxieties grow. Finally, the internal turmoil creates a sense of urgency that forces the salesperson to take one of two extreme actions: a coup de main or a full retreat from the account.

According to the *United States Department of Defense Dictionary*, a coup de main is a "swift attack that relies on speed and surprise to accomplish its objectives in a single blow."[5] A coup de main is a sudden, unexpected make-or-break strike against the enemy. The term literally means "strike with one's fist." In many ways a coup de main is an act of desperation, a lashing out against enemies or a conscious decision to bypass all established selection processes and customary sales etiquette to break out of a losing position.

It's natural to assume that the retreat position is the worst position to be in; however, this is not necessarily the case. Being in the retreat position actually is a double-edged sword. Because they have given up hope of winning the deal, salespeople in retreat won't spend any more time, resources, or mental anguish on the effort. In reality, the two most desirable positions to be in when the final selection is made are in the fortress or in retreat. All the salespeople in the other positions are still wasting their time.

BATTLEFIELD TACTICS BASED ON POSITION

Salespeople move from position to position as the sales cycle progresses. Moving from the coup de main to the escalade or reconnaissance position marks forward progress in the deal. Conversely, salespeople could experience setbacks that move them back to the coup de main position or dictate their retreat from the account.

The constant attack from competitors might weaken the leader's fortress walls over time and send him to the escalade position. A key customer contact might suddenly leave the company or be reassigned, forcing the salesperson from the reconnaissance position. A salesperson in the escalade position might never be able to establish anything more than a cordial relationship with the customer while his counterpart in the fortress enjoys a true friendship. This may force him to try a last-ditch effort to win with a coup de main.

A variety of battlefield tactics can be employed by salespeople in each of the various account positions. These tactics are either directed at the vendor in the fortress to lessen his leadership position or executed upon the customer to improve the salesperson's position in the account. While a variation of each tactic can be used in any of the five account positions, each tactic is placed in Figure 2.3 in its most commonly used location.

Fortress Tactics

Fortress tactics are based on using your unique customer relationship and your information advantage to stave off competitors and hold your leadership position. Here are some examples of fortress sales tactics.

PINCER ATTACK

In the Battle of Cannae in 216 B.C., the smaller Carthaginian army under the command of Hannibal defeated a numerically superior

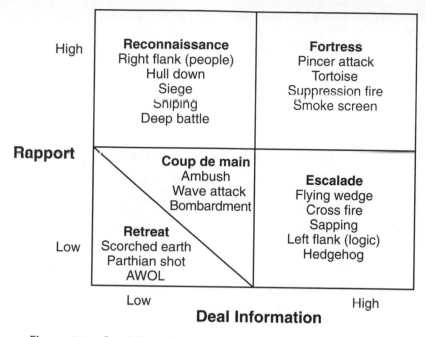

Figure 2.3 Battlefield Tactics Based on Position

Roman army using a pincer attack. Hannibal placed his weakest infantrymen in the middle of his line to give the impression of vulnerability while positioning his heavy infantrymen and cavalry on the flanks. As the battle progressed, his flanks closed on the Romans in a pinching motion. The result was annihilation: 60,000 Romans were killed compared to 6,000 Carthaginians.

In sales, the two pincers that crush your opponents are relationships and information. When customers like you personally and believe your product to be best (whether real or imagined), you are placed in the advantageous position of being able to control and edit the information flowing to and from the other vendors. This lopsided combination of personal friendships and information superiority are pincers that crush the competition. No tactic is more effective than the pincer attack.

TORTOISE

When Roman legionnaires attacked a walled city, they would use their shields in a formation known as a tortoise to protect themselves from arrows and missiles being hurled at them. The soldiers in the first row held their shields in front of them, the side rows held their shields to one side, and the rest of the soldiers held their shields above their heads so that the formation resembled a tortoise's shell.

In the sales equivalent of the tortoise tactic, advocates within an account form a shield to protect you from the slings and arrows of your competitors and from naysayers within the company. The strongest of these shields is provided by a senior executive—president, CEO, COO, or vice president—who is backing your solution. Regardless of your advocates' direct involvement in the selection process, the private opinions of these powerful people work behind the scenes to ward off known rivals and unseen internal detractors.

SUPPRESSION FIRE

The goal of suppression fire is to hold the enemy in check at its current position by firing as many rounds of ammunition as possible toward the enemy forces. Although the suppression fire is highly unlikely to kill the enemy forces, it will cause them to stay behind cover and eliminate their ability to attack.

The sales suppression fire we seek to create forces our adversaries to answer uncomfortable questions about their products, companies, and reputations. We want the customer to interrogate them about their faults on our behalf. At other times, we want to influence the sales cycle such that the customer creates unnecessary and unimportant steps that keep the other vendors busy.

SMOKE SCREEN

After Rome's liberation by Allied forces in June 1944, the German army was in full retreat from Italy, creating an opportune moment to destroy the withdrawing forces. The U.S. Army 141st First Battalion received orders to attack the retreating Germans. At 1:00 A.M. a battalion convoy moved out on the highway from Rome. Around 6:00 A.M. the convoy came under a devastating barrage of mortar, machine gun, artillery, and tank fire. One U.S. soldier would later say of the attack, "The Germans threw everything they had at us."[6]

The American battalion was pinned down along the highway in the worst possible position, out in the open. It was impossible for the soldiers to go forward or move backward. Finally, an hour after the attack began, a messenger made it back to the battalion command post and relayed the dire circumstances.

From the command post, mortars loaded with smoke bombs were fired at intervals of 25 yards between the German and American lines. As the black smoke rose from the shell bursts, it created a veil behind which the American forces were able to safely retreat. Although one hundred men were killed or wounded during the ambush, the battalion survived. The smoke screen saved their lives by concealing their movements.

Both salespeople and customers employ smoke screens to hide behind during the sales cycle. Salespeople schedule meetings to discuss product functionality when in reality they are using these meetings to discern the personal biases of decision makers. They provide customers with detailed information or technical specifications about their products' strengths in order to divert attention from the products' known weaknesses. During a meeting, they present the illusion of being calm and collected when they are really scared and nervous.

Customers hide the truth as well. In fact, the entire selection process is a smoke screen designed so that vendors never know exactly where they stand. Customers believe that creating this uncertainty is the best way to gain leverage over the vendors and ensure they receive the best attention, information, and most importantly, price.

Perhaps the greatest smoke screen of all is the RFP. Almost all RFPs are created with a favorite vendor in mind. Think about it for a moment. In order to create an RFP, the customer must have investigated the solutions that are available, studied the market position of each vendor, and most assuredly, met with certain vendors. Therefore, it's not surprising most RFPs include criteria that resemble one vendor's feature set or ask questions that the RFP creators know will cast particular solutions in a bad light. While all the responders put forth their best efforts to answer the RFP, in reality it is a smoke screen that has been laid down collectively by the customer and the favored vendor to camouflage the true nature of their relationship and the fact that the favorite already occupies the fortress position.

Reconnaissance Tactics

Reconnaissance tactics are all based on relationships—either taking advantage of existing relationships within an account or establishing new relationships to penetrate the fortress.

RIGHT FLANK (PEOPLE)

Heading into battle, armies are organized into formations. A division of 10,000 men might consist of two brigades, each composed of two regiments. Regardless of size, every formation has a left flank, center, and right flank. Perhaps the most common military tactic is to attack a formation at a flank, away from its center strength.

The right-flank sales tactic is associated with the people involved in the decision process. It is named after the right hemisphere of the brain, which is dominant for facial recognition, spatial abilities, and visual imagery. A right-flank movement is focused on finding "friendlies" within an account. Friendlies are individuals who seem to like you, are receptive to your position, and appreciate your company. For example, you might make a right-flank maneuver and bypass your main contact within an account in order to set up a meeting and establish a relationship with a more powerful decision maker.

HULL DOWN

The famous F-4 Sherman tank was the mainstay of Patton's Third Army. Because its armor was lighter and its profile higher than those of a German Panzer tank, one tactic that Sherman tankers would employ was called a "hull down." The driver would position the tank behind the crest of a hill or within a man-made ditch so that only the turret and cannon were exposed. The gunner would then fire away at enemy targets while the tank remained safely hidden. Salespeople employ the hull down tactic by enlisting a member of the selection team or other key influencer to disseminate positive information about their solution and negative information about competitors while they remain hidden in the background.

Here is a very simple example of a hull down. You see the CEO of the company you are trying to close a deal with having lunch with an industry consultant. You walk up to their table and tell the CEO that your product is the best solution on the market and his company should buy it. What would his response be? Most likely he would be skeptical at the very least. But let's suppose you had asked the consultant beforehand to casually recommend your product to the CEO over lunch. The CEO's response to your pitch would be the opposite.

SIEGE

The siege tactic is an attrition-based strategy for conquering a fortress or city. A siege is both a conventional and a psychological operation. Daily supplies are blocked, causing shortages of basic necessities, while the stress of being surrounded and under threat of imminent attack weakens the defenders' resolve to hold out. Laying siege to a fortress or city is usually not the first choice of action by any military commander because it ties up large numbers of troops and other resources for long periods of time. Rather, it is a last resort after other battlefield tactics have failed.

In one sense, all salespeople lay siege to the accounts they are working on. However, many salespeople are experts at employing the siege strategy in a less conventional way. Contrary to common sense, they actually hound the customer into purchasing their solution. They will not abandon the account or leave the decision makers alone until the customer buys. Relentless, unapologetic hounding and stalking of the customer are central to the siege tactic.

SNIPING

Snipers are hated by infantries of all armies for good reason. From their well-hidden positions, snipers evoke fear. A single sniper can pin down an entire platoon and inflict many casualties. One U.S. Marine sniper had 93 confirmed kills in Vietnam, the longest at 2,500 yards from his target.[7] That's 25 football fields away!

In sales, not everyone on the customer's selection committee will be enamored with you and your solution. People will eagerly voice their opinions in the selection process. Usually, the venting of opinions, both good and bad, about your product will result in a healthy debate that is necessary for the committee to reach a consensus. However, occasionally an individual may be so ardently opposed to you and your company that that person must be taken out of the selection process altogether. The tactic to use in this situation is sniping.

The most effective sales sniping involves lying in wait for the perfect moment to discredit and take out a detractor. Let's assume, for example, that a member of the selection team has consistently harangued you during the sales process about your product's lack of a particular capability. In reality, his adamant opposition is just a red herring (an irrelevant topic presented to divert attention) to hide his personal bias toward another competitor. Meanwhile, after meeting individually with the other selection team members, you discover this capability isn't considered crucial. When you meet with the entire selection team again, you will want to get this issue out on the table and talked about openly so that the detractor is essentially "sniped" by the other committee members.

Sometimes sniping can get very personal. For example, a lower-level employee who is voicing opinions against you must be removed from the sales process. Taking advantage of your relationships with executives, you attack the subordinate's credentials, credibility, and capabilities. You instill fear in the executives that the project will be unsuccessful with this person on the team.

Usually, sniping is very uncomfortable to do. At times during customer meetings, you must dominate detractors and silence their opposition in order to maintain your momentum. While we tend to become more emotional when we are challenged, the most effective sniper remains calm. Whether you use a logical argument to contradict a detractor's claim, give a customer example to repudiate an antagonistic statement, or expose the ridiculousness of the objection itself, a composed response is far more effective than an emotional one.

DEEP BATTLE

During the cold war, in anticipation of a Russian attack in central Europe, the U.S. military developed the military doctrine referred to as "deep battle." Deep battle would synchronize the actions of ground troops fighting on the front to air operations simultaneously attacking the rear, deep in Russian territory. Deep battle was based on the "see deep, strike deep" concept. According to Colonel William G. Hanne of the Strategic Studies Institute, "The linchpin to the entire operational concept is accurate and timely intelligence on enemy forces, the terrain, and the weather."[8]

Deep battle is an appropriate sales tactic when you sense a selection committee is aligned against you and fear its recommendation to senior management. The goal of deep battle is to use a "spy"—a friend on the inside—to introduce you to the ultimate and final decision maker, who exists in every account. (We'll talk about the "bully with the juice" in detail in the next chapter.) You want a chance to plead your case in person.

Since you need to bypass the evaluation steps laid out by the selection committee, you must have excellent intelligence and a very strong spy to execute deep battle. If the tactic is successful, you will have neutralized the selection committee's power and have a chance to win the deal. If the tactic fails (which is often the case), you will have alienated the committee and therefore lost. However, knowing you have lost the deal is actually a blessing in disguise. Controlling your destiny, as opposed to bowing to the demands of a biased committee, will save you from wasting precious time and effort on an account where you just can't win.

Escalade Tactics

Escalade tactics are based on information and logic, and their purpose is to create a psychological advantage. They can be used to appeal to the customer's deductive reasoning or effect fear, uncertainty, and doubt in the customer's mind.

FLYING WEDGE

The flying wedge formation has been used by Roman legionnaires, B-26 bombers over Germany, and mechanized forces in the war in Iraq. The flying wedge is a concentrated battle formation focused on one point. The attacking force forms into a triangle to breach the enemy's line at a single spot. Once a gap is created in the enemy's line, the formation expands and pushes out in different directions.

Here's a sales example of the flying wedge. Let's say you have advantageous benchmark information that shows your product is faster than your opponent's solution, which happens to be in the lead. At every possible opportunity, you harangue the customer about the implications of poor performance, the technical differences between the products that cause poor performance, how much unnecessary equipment would need to be purchased to rectify the performance problem, and the business impact of poor performance. You continually hammer upon performance in order to create an opening, a wedge or gap between the leader and the customer, where you can begin to spread your company's story and your product's benefits to the decision makers.

CROSS FIRE

The U.S. Marines' battle against Japanese soldiers on the island of Iwo Jima was described as a "graveyard for the dead and hell for the living."[9] The assault on Hill 382, nicknamed "the Meat Grinder," was especially deadly. Japanese machine gunners were positioned so that they could unleash deadly fire upon anyone attempting to take the hill. Artillery positioned across the island atop Mount Suribachi could fire on the advancing Marines from any direction. The cross fire created a killing ground, and in one day alone, 492 marines lost their lives trying to take the Meat Grinder.

In sales, the cross fire tactic involves using other people to help you win a deal. It may include other members of your company, such as your technical system engineer, sales manager, or business partners, who have a vested interest in your winning. You fire away at the competition together. It's a logic-based sales tactic designed to cause doubt in the customer's mind about another vendor's capabilities while bolstering your position.

SAPPING

The trench warfare of World War I reduced the fighting to a stalemate. To end the standoff, British army engineers began tunneling (sapping) underneath the German trenches at Messines Ridge in Belgium. After about two years of digging, the sappers placed 450 tons of high explosives in 21 different mines. When the explosives were detonated, approximately 10,000 German troops were killed. The sound from the blast was the loudest man-made noise ever heard.

Perhaps the most effective sales example of sapping is telling a prospect about customers who have dumped the competition's products and switched to yours. Even a competitor who is safely in the confines of the fortress can have the lead position sapped from beneath him by these enormously destructive stories.

LEFT FLANK (LOGIC)

Whereas the right-flank tactic is based on people, the left-flank tactic is based on logic and information. Flanking to the left refers to the tactic of changing the customer's selection criteria or raising a critical issue the customer is unaware of. It is named after the left side of the brain, the part that is analytical and invokes rational reasoning and deductive logic.

The right- and left-flank tactics work together. For instance, a meeting can be set up under the guise of one topic when the goal is really to gain access to a specific person (right flank) and influence that person to change the logical selection criteria (left flank).

HEDGEHOG

The hedgehog is a defensive tactic used offensively. Military units will employ a hedgehog defense scheme to protect a large area from attack when they don't have enough manpower to defend it conventionally. Soldiers are spread out into carefully placed positions and dig in, or "hedgehog." When the attackers encounter hedgehogs, they naturally funnel into the open spaces between them. While the attackers believe they are making progress, they are now subject to fire from other hedgehogs.

An effective hedgehog defense in sales is to spread out and lengthen the selection process. Contrary to the common-sense thinking that it is always best to shorten the sales cycle, sometimes it is necessary to make it longer by inserting steps the customer didn't think about or ask for.

Slowing down the sales cycle can create problems for the vendor in the fortress. Offering to complete a detailed on-site study of the customer's business, inviting the customer to make site visits to other installations, and taking the customer on a tour of your corporate headquarters are great examples of hedgehogs. These hedgehog events allow you to demonstrate your expertise, and they give you additional time to build the personal relationships you need to win.

Coup de Main Tactics

Coup de main tactics are risky, dangerous tactics that have a tendency to backfire. Therefore, keep them in reserve until late in the sales cycle for use in the event you are so far behind your competitors that you have nothing to lose.

AMBUSH

In the wild, a predator ambushes its prey by making a surprise attack from a hiding place. As simple as this may sound, military ambushes are quite complex and require careful planning to succeed. The ambush location must be a place the enemy passes predictably, and it must offer concealment and an easy escape route.

The two types of military ambushes have different goals: one is to kidnap troops for interrogation purposes, while the other is to eliminate troops altogether. The soldiers chosen to execute either type must be briefed on the plan, know where their counterparts are so they don't inadvertently hurt them, and be equipped with the right weapons to get the job done. Finally, the ambushers must have patience and lie in wait for the precise moment to attack. When they do attack, the attack cannot be done halfheartedly; it must occur at full force.

In sales, the ambush of competitors is just as complex. Which competitor are we out to ambush? What type of ambush will we execute? Will we lie in wait until that competitor makes a statement we know we can clearly contradict and ruin its reputation in the process? Will we take the initiative and instill fear and doubt in the customer's mind? Or will we take a consultative approach as the customer's trusted adviser and set a trap?

How will we carry out the ambush? Are we going to tell the customer about a new, unreleased product; provide third-party objective opinions; or disclose negative information about a competitor based upon our own experiences? When will the ambush occur? Will it be during the big sales presentation on the third PowerPoint slide or in an informal meeting with the customer? Who will execute the ambush? Will it be the salesperson, his manager, his presales engineer, or all of them together? Finally, what is our backup plan and what countermeasures will we take if our ambush fails?

Above all, a successful ambush requires detailed planning. These are just a few of the questions that need to be answered before attempting one.

WAVE ATTACK

During the Korean War, the Communist army frequently fought United Nations forces using the wave attack. It would send wave after wave of poorly equipped soldiers straight at the UN positions in a direct attack. The North Korean commanders who ordered these attacks knew the casualties would be high and the likelihood of success was low. Therefore, they employed the wave attack only as a last resort when other types of attacks had proven unsuccessful.

The sales equivalent of the wave attack is similarly accomplished by throwing bodies at an account. A salesperson may ask the president, vice president of sales, and other senior executives from within his company to blindly call their counterparts at the customer's company. The salesperson may ask his technical support team (system engineers, consultants, and analysts) to establish relationships with key contacts to find out information and influence opinions and criteria. Done at the right time in the sales cycle, the wave attack is an appropriate strategy.

However, attempting the wave attack late in the sales cycle is usually a waste of time. Selection team members don't like it when vendors go over their heads and call their boss or their boss's boss. Worse, an ill-timed wave attack can be a fatal career move for the salesperson as it allows the senior leaders within the salesperson's company to be eyewitnesses to his failings and shortcomings.

BOMBARDMENT

Strategic bombing is the precision bombing of high-value military targets (such as command-and-control centers) and industrial targets (such as factories and railroads). The bombardments may occur from high, medium, and low altitudes. This tactic undermines a nation's ability to win wars.

In the sales vernacular, bombardment refers to the tactic of sending a constant stream of technical information, business justification material, and company marketing propaganda to the various levels of personnel within the account you are trying to win. The material sent to the senior executive level is quite different from the information sent to midlevel managers and low-level personnel. Senior executives should receive short, high-level summary information, such as press articles or one-page reviews. Midlevel managers should be sent more detailed case studies from other successful customers and analysts' white papers. Low-level, hands-on product evaluators should receive data sheets, user manuals, and detailed implementation guides.

Bombardment is an excellent beachhead tactic to use when you are trying to develop some recognition and credibility with particular individuals before you contact them personally. As opposed to the wave attack, where many colleagues are involved, bombardment is executed solely by the salesperson, so it's far more efficient and far less risky.

Retreat Tactics

It takes a lot of discipline to walk away from an account that has involved a heavy investment of time, energy, and emotions. Knowing how to retreat from an account where there is little chance of winning is just as important as knowing when to stop working on the deal. Each of the three different types of retreat tactics is used to accomplish a different purpose.

SCORCHED EARTH

Napoleon Bonaparte successfully employed scorched-earth retreats against the British in Spain and on the Russian front. In recognition of his impending defeat, he destroyed everything that could have been of value to the approaching British and Russian armies.

A scorched-earth sales tactic involves using any means necessary to stop the deal from happening. At this point you are not trying to win the deal anymore; you are only trying to prevent the other vendors from winning. This is an extreme measure of last resort. Examples include calling the customer's senior management and explaining that the selection process was biased because decision makers had improper relationships with the winning vendor; complaining to interested outside parties (regulatory boards, media outlets, financial investors, and the general public) about misconduct during the selection process; seeking legal action to stop the purchase; and offering to provide your product at a greatly reduced price or even for free.

PARTHIAN SHOT

Ancient Parthian horse archers employed an interesting tactic to harass their enemies. They would start to retreat from the enemy at full gallop, then stop and turn sharply to fire their arrows. The term *parting shot* refers to this tactic.

In sales, a Parthian shot is a sharp, telling remark or critical communication made by a retreating salesperson to strike a blow at the decision makers' confidence. Examples include warnings about failed customer installations, critical memorandums sent to executives about the selection team members' competence, or predictions about the future failure of the project.

AWOL

Absent without leave (AWOL) is a military term for soldiers who are away from their posts or military duties without permission. Soldiers who go AWOL have no intention of deserting the military permanently. Rather, they are abandoning their responsibilities temporarily.

In sales, it quite often makes sense for salespeople who suspect they are losing to go AWOL and disappear. Doing so forces an interested customer to pursue the salesperson. For example, when the customer asks for information, the salesperson will not provide it until he gets the information or commitments he wants in return. Doing nothing sometimes frustrates the members of the selection team who are working against the salesperson as it forces them to spend additional time dealing with this disruptive person. Other times, it is exactly what they would like to have happen. They want the salesperson and his solution to quietly disappear.

INDIVIDUAL BATTLEFIELD TACTIC CASE STUDY

Here's a story about one of Tricia's accounts showing how she employed the indirect strategy to turn a very difficult prospect into a customer. From a tactical standpoint, Tricia right-flanked to get inside the fortress. Once inside the fortress, she launched a pincer attack and continually laid down suppression fire upon the other competitors.

Paul was the manager in charge of information systems security at a well-known financial services company. His main responsibility was to ensure that customers' data was safe and secure. The position held a lot of responsibility and commanded equal authority. A breach in a customer's data could have significant financial implications. In addition to the legal liability, the resulting unfavorable press coverage would have a great impact on the company.

Paul was a tough-minded authoritarian. He didn't meet with vendors; rather, he verbally abused them in front of his staff. These staged events were designed to showcase his considerable knowledge and the extent of his authority. Paul didn't trust anybody. He spoke negatively about other divisions of his company and how he would manage them differently.

Developing Paul into a "spy" and internal champion was critical. If Tricia didn't win him over, she wouldn't win the deal. She knew it was pointless to argue with Paul as there was nothing to be gained by doing so. He would not be swayed by any vendor's logic or reason and would resist these frontal attacks. A direct approach based on logic or reason wouldn't work with him. However, an indirect approach based on Paul's human nature would—if Tricia could understand his true motivations and desires.

Paul would choose the solution he believed was in his own best interest. So what did Paul want? He wanted to be a hero. He wanted to prove he was a smart businessman. He was seeking the recognition he felt he was entitled to. Tricia's mission was to ensure that the selection of her product helped Paul achieve his goals. Therefore, she would have to tactically right-flank Paul in order to get inside the fortress.

Paul was considering replacing the company's existing security vendor because of continual product stability problems and the poor quality of its support. The product had been purchased before Paul was hired, and the company had spent a significant amount of money implementing it.

Tricia worked with her management to package a very compelling proposal that included product trade-in credits and implementation services. This excited Paul. He would take great pride in boasting to his managers how he not only fixed the problem but essentially got their money back, too. At this point, Tricia successfully moved into the fortress.

Tricia continually sold to Paul's ego. At every opportunity, she elicited Paul's feedback, not so much for its own merits but rather so Paul could hear himself talk about her solution. She spoke to him daily and provided updates on competitors that Paul would use in his conversations with them (suppression fire). Next she executed a two-pronged pincer tactic to solidify her position. She arranged for Paul to meet with others from her company—the technical support manager, the product management team, and various members of the executive staff. Tricia even arranged for Paul to be invited to join her company's customer advisory committee. These fact-finding sessions and personal meetings with executives deepened Paul's commitment to the company. Meanwhile, the other vendors were locked out of the fortress since they could not build relationships with Paul nor did they have a chance to disseminate their product information.

Paul would ultimately become a fantastic "spy" and an incredible champion. He was sold on Tricia's company as well as the product. Finally, someone was treating him with the respect he deserved. Later, he even seriously considered joining Tricia's company. Paul wasn't such a tough guy after all.

It would have been pointless and probably even detrimental to Tricia's sales efforts to try to convince Paul on a point-by-point basis why her solution was superior. Based on Paul's nature, his company's history, and its current situation, the only way to win Paul over and close this deal was with an indirect approach.

COMPANY BATTLEFIELD TACTIC CASE STUDY

The indirect strategy and associated battlefield tactics apply to companies just as well as they do to salespeople. In 1991, Informix Software was just one of a dozen relational database software suppliers. All of these vendors were competing against Oracle, the 800-pound gorilla, and the market's number two player, technically sophisticated Sybase. In only four years, Informix Software was able to move past all these companies and challenge Oracle's dominance. This truly remarkable use of the indirect strategy is well worth studying today. (For a comprehensive review of the Informix story, read *The Real Story of Informix Software and Phil White: Lessons in Business and Leadership for the Executive Team* by Steve W. Martin [Sand Hill Publishing, 2005].)

Selling for Informix was grueling hand-to-hand combat. Oracle used a direct approach based on superiority in numbers. When Oracle made a sales call it would typically "unload the bus." This sales strategy term, made famous by IBM, involves bringing in as many people as possible on a sales call to show your depth, breadth, and market dominance.

In addition to the local salesperson and sales management, Oracle would bring database presales engineers, application development tools engineers, experts from its business accounting applications, industry marketing specialists from whichever vertical industry the prospect was a part of (manufacturing, retail, consumer packaged goods, government, and so on), and consultants who would help implement the software. This show of strength was impressive, and companies that were used to dealing with IBM responded positively, as expected.

Sybase presented an entirely different set of challenges for Informix. Sybase was the darling of the industry, loved by the analyst community. The industry publications also proclaimed Sybase's technical superiority, which was true at that time. Sybase had key technical features that Oracle and Informix didn't offer.

For many years, Informix had tried to go toe-to-toe against Oracle and Sybase. But Informix was outnumbered by Oracle 10 to 1, and it couldn't make a frontal assault based on technical functionality against Sybase. The only way to defeat these better-equipped companies was to use the indirect strategy.

Picking the right battles to fight was the secret of sales success at Informix. The company adopted an indirect approach based on attacking the enemy's weaknesses in order to dislodge Oracle and Sybase from the fortress. Informix could win in four areas: applications, hardware partners, Unix operating system zealots, and education of the ignored.

Informix executed a hull down strategy to attack the fortress from the reconnaissance quadrant by recruiting several hundred independent software companies to create their applications using the Informix database. In general, these solutions were not the popular enterprise software solutions available at the time, which were based on Oracle and Sybase. These independent software companies were niche players that had developed small applications for specific vertical industries, such as hotel property management, higher education accounting, or legal office automation. These applications seeded accounts with Informix's products.

Another reconnaissance quadrant tactic Informix used was to right-flank the competition and establish relationships with the outcasts and ignored. "People don't buy from people they have never met" was an important Informix concept. Therefore,

Informix salespeople went out of their way to meet and educate potential customers about Unix and Informix. The goal at Informix was to be the first database salesperson to start a relationship with a customer.

To move from the escalade position into the fortress, Informix employed the cross fire tactic and established partnerships with computer hardware manufacturers. Hewlett-Packard, Sun Microsystems, IBM, and Digital Equipment Corporation were the major hardware players of the day. Unfortunately, they were much more interested in working with Oracle and Sybase than with Informix. However, Informix developed reseller relationships with second-tier players such as Sequent, Pyramid, Unisys, Data General, AT&T, NCR Corporation, and Group Bull. Their salespeople were eager to work with the Informix sales force and introduce them into their accounts.

Informix aggressively courted and sold to Unix zealots in order to ambush Oracle and Sybase from the coup de main position. Unix purists loved Informix. Usually, these people were low-level technical geeks within a customer's information technology department. Oracle and Sybase would consciously ignore them. Although selling at low levels is risky, surprisingly often these low-level technical people were the ultimate decision makers. Informix befriended them, whereas Oracle salespeople ran over them in their haste to get into the office of the vice president of information technology.

The entire Informix sales force adopted a new demeanor, based on the indirect strategy, to differentiate themselves from Oracle and Sybase. Informix's salespeople were truly friendly and responsive when compared to the aristocratic Sybase salespeople and the slick Oracle salespeople in cufflinks and monogrammed dress shirts. In essence, Informix was the kinder, nicer, and easier-to-deal-with company, not because it necessarily wanted to be but because the circumstances of the day dictated it.

The results of the indirect strategy were quite impressive. Within two years of its adoption, Informix stock was ranked number one for return on equity in the Silicon Valley Top 150. By 1995, Informix had overtaken Sybase as the number one challenger to Oracle, and Informix's stock was named the top five-year performer by the *Wall Street Journal*. Informix's revenues would reach $1 billion in 1996.

When undermanned and technically outclassed, you must wage war indirectly. You must carefully choose the battles you fight and be first to the fight. It also makes no sense for the underdog to fight the battle alone, so partnerships must be established. Utilizing the indirect strategy was the only way for Informix to compete with the behemoth Oracle and technically superior Sybase.

CLOSING THOUGHTS

In this chapter we introduced the concept that the grand strategy of selling your product should be based on the indirect strategy of selling to the human nature of customers. We also reviewed the components of the grand strategy: battles and battlefield maneuvers. While the grand strategy should always be based on the indirect approach, battles can be either indirectly or directly fought. Battlefield maneuvers are usually direct.

Let's examine a fictitious deal from the standpoint of two different salespeople. A company has formed a selection committee to buy some new business machinery. The selection committee consists of four members and is headed by a department vice president. The committee has documented the selection process, technical needs, and business requirements.

A salesperson working on this account using a direct grand strategy would follow the customer's instructions and adhere to the selection process. Conversely, a salesperson using an indirect grand strategy would work on the account quite differently. He might have had input in creating the requirements or developed a special relationship with the committee leader or another member ahead of time.

The salesperson employing the direct strategy would say his goal is to have his solution selected by the committee members. The salesperson subscribing to the indirect strategy would say his goal is to win over the vice president who heads the selection committee, thereby rendering the committee's decision moot.

The indirect approach has inherent beauty. Although the following e-mail I received may seem quite elementary, it demonstrates the subtleness and impact of the indirect strategy.

> I sell copywriting services by trade, and one day, I visited an equipment company that was about to introduce a new newspaper text processing system into the market. They were evaluating various copywriters who would be hired to write the brochure about the system. As always, I had to sit around in the lobby for a while, but eventually I was ushered into the manager's office, given a cup of coffee, and told to do my stuff (showtime!!!).
>
> I have always been nervous about doing presentations so I have developed the habit of getting prospective clients to talk about themselves, their companies, and their products first. As they talk, I would interject a comment to show my mastery of advertising and marketing (and perhaps even their business).
>
> Well, at this particular company the fellow I met with talked on and on, with me interjecting an occasional comment for over an hour. When he finally ran out of things to say, he just asked me how much the brochure was going to cost and when I could start working on it. He didn't ask for references. He never even asked to see my portfolio. He just wanted to get on with it and get the brochure done.[10]

Why is this story important? All Jim, the copywriter, did was listen to the customer's oration for an hour and make a comment here and there. That's the point. An inexperienced salesperson would have interrupted the customer to give his canned presentation, when it was actually unnecessary. Likewise, an egotistical salesperson might have thought he could not earn the business unless he changed the topic of conversation to himself. An impatient salesperson might have thrust his portfolio upon the customer, thereby presenting the customer with the opportunity to disapprove. A more dominant salesperson might have asked himself what he was doing there. Why should he have to listen to this guy drone on and on? He would interrupt (and insult) the manager to give his opinion why he should be selected.

All of these salespeople would have defaulted to selling with a direct approach, putting themselves first! Jim chose the indirect approach and put the customer first by listening as he spoke cathartically. Although you may think he didn't actually do anything, Jim's listening was the indirect approach to winning. As Sun Tzu said, "Supreme excellence consists of breaking the enemy's resistance without fighting."[11] That's what makes this deal so beautiful: Jim didn't have to fight any battles with other competitors or the customer over price.

CHAPTER 3

The Five Steps to Victory

The general who wins a battle makes many calculations in his temple before the battle is fought. The general who loses a battle makes but few calculations beforehand.

—SUN TZU
The Art of War

I n *The Art of War*, Sun Tzu recounts the story of Tien Tan, the leader of the army defending the city of Chi-mo against its arch-enemy, the Yens.[1] With the Yens encamped around Chi-mo, Tien Tan called the townspeople together and told them that he feared the Yen army would cut off the noses of the Chi-mo prisoners they held. He told the crowd that if the Yens carried out this heinous act, it would surely be the undoing of their city. When the Yens heard about his comments, they proceeded to cut off the prisoners' noses. However, the city did not fall. Instead, the Yens' actions united the citizens of Chi-mo to defend the city in a spirit as never before.

Tien Tan then sent double agents to the Yen camp. The spies delivered false reports saying that what Tien Tan dreaded most was that the Yens would dig up the Chi-mo ancestral tombs outside the city. Again, the Yens followed his suggestion and dug up the family graves. The enraged citizens watched from atop the walls surrounding the city as the Yens burned the corpses. Now the entire city was eager to fight and kill the Yens.

Next, Tien Tan replaced the regular soldiers who usually manned the walls with older and weaker men and women. Then he sent 20,000 ounces of silver with a note from the city's wealthy citizens asking the Yen leader to spare their homes and families when the city fell. The Yen leader replied he would. Falling into the trap, the overconfident Yens thought victory would be easy and grew lax and negligent of their own security.

Later that night, Tien Tan launched his attack. One thousand oxen were stampeded into the Yen camp with five thousand warriors close behind. At the same time, the entire population of Chi-mo shrieked and banged drums and pots, creating a clangorous noise. The Yens were caught off guard. During the fighting, the Yen general was slain and the Yen soldiers who weren't killed fled in disarray. The attack was a complete success because of Tien Tan's carefully thought-out plan.

Five important lessons from Tien Tan's victory are directly applicable to achieving sales victories. First, Tien Tan set the tempo of the conflict. He didn't wait for the Yens to attack. He proactively executed his plan, even though he was initially at a disadvantage. Second, he focused on human nature. He won over the hearts and minds of the citizens of Chi-mo and played mental games with the Yens. Third, spies played a critical role in gathering information and disseminating misinformation. Without them, Tien Tan would not have won. Fourth, he understood the organization of the enemy. His plan of attack was devised with it in mind. Fifth, a key part of his strategy was to go after the Yen leader. In this chapter we will discuss how these five key points are necessary steps to obtain our sales victories.

STEP 1—SET THE TEMPO

What would you have done if you had been in charge of the city of Chi-mo and were surrounded by the enemy? The natural inclination would be to bolster your defensive position and fortify the city. However, Tien Tan decided to take the offensive. By doing so, he set the tempo for the battle.

The best way to set the tempo for any battle is to be the first on the battlefield. The one who arrives first can survey the surroundings and identify the best places to establish fighting positions. He has more time to map out a plan for the battle. The one who arrives later must first react to the incumbent's moves before he can initiate any offensive movements himself.

If you work for an underdog company that competes for sales against the industry leader, setting the tempo for a battle is a critical concept. How do you defeat the market leader? According to Napoleon, "The art of war is to gain time when your strength is inferior."[2] Let's take a moment to analyze his profound saying.

As a general rule, it is always best to be the first salesperson in an account. The chance to understand a customer's environment first, establish relationships, and set the criteria for the selection process are obvious advantages. If you are the first salesperson in the account, the only obstacle that can prevent you from successfully completing your strategy is the customer.

However, it's not always possible to find a customer first, and sometimes arriving first doesn't even matter. What matters is the strength of your position versus that of the competition. You can define your strength compared to your competitor's in one of three ways: you have the advantage, you are equal, or you are outclassed. And the three basic types of strengths are relationship (the personal relationships you have built in the account), product (the technical merits of your product and the associated perception of your company in the marketplace), and personnel (the quality and quantity of people who are at your disposal to work on the account).

Defining your account strength can be tricky for two reasons. First, your marketing department's job is to pump out volumes of propaganda proclaiming that every aspect of the company and its product is superior to the competition. Therefore, your product's true strength can be ascertained only with direct customer feedback gained in past sales cycles. This is one important reason to do postmortems on why you lost business (a subject we'll discuss in Chapter 6).

The second reason is a little more complex, so perhaps it's best to explain it using an analogy. Let's say you asked World War II veterans from Russia, Japan, Germany, Britain, and America which army had the best soldiers. Even though the veterans include both winners and losers of the war, they would most likely answer that their country's soldiers were best. Those who lost the war might say it was because of inferior weaponry or lack of resources. Those who won would say it was because of their fighting prowess and skill. In many ways, this is similar to how salespeople view themselves and their organizations. Whereas salespeople will say they are directly responsible for winning, the natural tendency is to blame losses on something else. In essence, the sales organization's esprit de corps ultimately taints judgments. The true strength of your competitive position directly correlates to the percentage of deals you win.

The only way to accurately gauge how you stack up personally against the enemy is in head-to-head confrontations. Therefore, you must make it a point to know which salesperson from the competition is working on the account. It's not enough to know you are competing against XYZ Company. You want to know you are competing against John Smith, the local salesperson from XYZ Company. This information is relatively easy to find out, but most salespeople don't even ask. You can ask the customer the question outright or soften it by saying, "I've run into John Smith of XYZ Company occasionally" and waiting for a response.

The decision on whether to pursue an account can be a difficult one. One deciding factor is who has set the tempo in the account—you or another competitor. This is particularly important when your product has a long sales cycle that requires a large investment of your time and your company's resources. Basing the decision on an honest assessment of competitive strength is critical. For example, you should pursue accounts where you have established personal relationships. If you enjoy product and personnel advantages, you should almost always pursue an account, even if you are late into the deal. If you have product and personnel disadvantages, you must be first into the account to win. If you are on equal footing with the competition, you must be on time at the start of the evaluation process in order to build the relationship advantage. Figure 3.1 illustrates the tempo rules (when you should arrive in accounts) when your products and personnel are superior, equal, or inferior to your competitor's.

Obviously, many combinations are possible. The decision to work on an account or walk away from it shouldn't be made solely by the salesperson; it's always best to get outsiders' opinions. The best people to help you make this call are your sales manager and the other members of your team who would work on the account with you. Not only is the personnel attribute a comparison of you against the salesperson you are competing directly against, but it also involves the availability, quality, and commitment of your team members (technical presales support, consultants, and management) to win the account. Therefore, it makes sense to get their buy-in before you move forward on any account.

Once you're engaged in the deal, setting the tempo takes on a new meaning. While a good defense may keep you in the deal, the

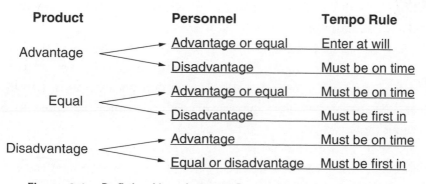

Product		Personnel	Tempo Rule
Advantage		Advantage or equal	Enter at will
		Disadvantage	Must be on time
Equal		Advantage or equal	Must be on time
		Disadvantage	Must be first in
Disadvantage		Advantage	Must be on time
		Equal or disadvantage	Must be first in

Figure 3.1 Defining Your Account Strengths versus a Competitor's

only way to win is to be on the offense. However, the other competitors also want to control the tempo of the deal and execute their offensive plans. Meanwhile, the customer wants to dictate the steps that will be taken during the selection process and control each of the various vendors to prevent them from running slipshod through the company.

Setting the tempo is the first step in winning the war. Never forget, the only two appropriate positions to be in at the end of the deal are first place, as the winner, or last place, as the first loser. Every place in between is the result of a judgment error. Timing plays an important role in every account. In the words of Napoleon Bonaparte, "I may lose a battle but I will never lose a minute."[3]

STEP 2—FOCUS ON HUMAN NATURE (WINNING HEARTS *AND* MINDS)

George Patton said, "Wars may be fought with weapons but they are won by men. It is the spirit of the men who follow and the man who leads that gains victory."[4] Patton's comment applies to sales just as much as it does to war. The spirit of the salesperson is far more important than the feature checklist of a product. Besides, most of the competing products in today's marketplace are relatively equal in the customers' eyes.

It would be a cliché to say you must be positive and enthusiastic while you explain your product's features, benefits, and specifications to a customer. Since all your competitors are just as friendly and positive as you are, the spirit needed for victory requires something more.

Selling requires capturing the hearts and minds of customers based on a strategy that takes into account the emotions of the decision maker as well as the logical reasons to buy. Customers aren't completely logical decision makers in the real world. The final decision-making process is a blend of human nature and logical rationalization. At the foundation of all sales is a relationship between people. The interaction between these people, the intangible part of the sales process, is ultimately responsible for the decision being made. Logic and reason play secondary roles.

Customers do not establish vendor relationships based on the best business judgment; rather, they judge vendors based on who establishes the best business relationships. A customer I recently interviewed as part of a blind survey said it best: "We made it clear that we weren't buying a brochure or data sheet. For that matter, we weren't even buying a product. We were buying a long-term relationship with another company and, equally important, the team of people from that company with whom we would have to work on a day in, day out basis."

The grand strategy of selling your product is based on the indirect strategy of selling to human nature. Figure 3.2 illustrates the three components of selling to human nature: customers' psychological needs and customers' opinions of you and your competitors.

On the left-hand side of the block are benefactions, the customers' psychological needs. The term *benefaction* refers to the psychological benefits that determine a person's actions. Customers purchase products that increase their happiness, esteem, power, or wealth. They rationalize these psychological decisions with logic and facts. For example, a vice president of a manufacturing company may explain that he wants to buy a new conveyor system because it will save a million dollars a year when in reality he is making the purchase to show the CEO that he is a prudent businessman and fiscally conservative. The desire to impress the CEO (the benefit) drives the conveyor system purchase (the action).

Four core psychological drives determine selection behavior. These four benefactions are physical well-being, pain avoidance, self-preservation, and self-gratification.

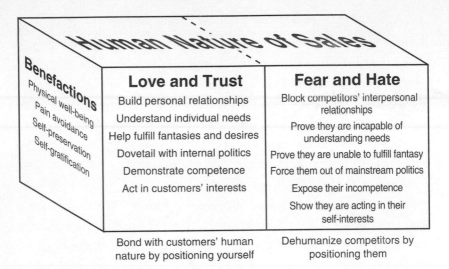

Figure 3.2   Indirect Strategy of the Human Nature of Sales

Physical well-being, the will to survive, is one of our strongest desires. It weighs heavily in the minds of both customers and competitors. Making customers feel their jobs are safe in your hands is a top priority. Ideally, you would like them to believe (whether it is true or not) that the competitive solutions are actually threats to their livelihood. Maneuvering the competitors into a life-threatening position in an account such that they are forced to make a direct attack on you will bolster your claims.

When something is hurting you badly, the desire to eliminate the source of pain can be all-consuming. Pain is one of the best purchase motivators because customers are forced to act quickly and decisively to eliminate it. Similarly, a salesperson who is being harangued by his boss about a longstanding account that won't close is experiencing pain. You must exploit both of these pains, often by controlling the tempo of the sales cycle. Sometimes it makes sense to speed up the sales cycle, and at other times it is better to slow it down. For example, quickly assembling a

SWAT team of personnel and showing how you can solve a customer's distressing situation will lock out the competition. Conversely, slowing down the sales cycle can cause a frustrated opponent to make a rash mistake.

We naturally seek the approval of others. Self preservation, the desire to be recognized for our unique talents while still belonging to a group, applies to customers and salespeople alike. Customers purchase items that they believe will enhance their stature and protect their group position. Salespeople want to be the pack leaders.

Everyone has a selfish ego, and self-gratification is our desire to put our own needs before everyone else's. Customers will go to great lengths to purchase something that makes them feel better about themselves and superior to others. Egos drive the business world. Unfortunately, most salespeople are taught to sell solutions based on customer pain when, in fact, ego and self-preservation are usually the real motivators behind large enterprise sales.

The following list reveals the true reasons why customers buy your product. It's not your product's performance, ease of use, or efficiency that customers are in love with. It's you. Therefore, your priorities should be to earn their love and trust by understanding their personal needs, desires, and fantasies. You must know if they are just trying to hold onto their job, prop up their importance, or bring about a long-awaited promotion. Once you understand these desires, you become part of the customers' political landscape, aligned with the decision-making process. Consider these customer statements:

- I'm risk averse.

- I'm skeptical of the other vendor.

- I like to be part of a group.

- I want the security of a marketable skill.

- I want that promotion.

- I want to keep my job.

- I'm worried about the competition.

- I am tired of working hard.

- I like new challenges.

- I want to please others.

- I want to be important.

- I want to make a difference.

- I like you!

Your grand strategy is to dehumanize the enemy by differentiating yourself personally. In other words, you want customers to view you as the only person who can address their personal needs, solve their business problems, and help them achieve their career hopes and life's desires. You want them to sincerely believe that you are the only person who is truly acting in their best interests.

People connect with others very quickly, and first impressions can have a long-term impact. Customers tend to make snap judgments early in the sales cycle based on whom they like and respect. By demonstrating your competence, you expose your competitor's incompetence. Knowing the details of how your product works and being able to answer customers' questions about your company are obviously vital parts of sales. However, the real questions to answer honestly are, "Compared to the salespeople I am competing with, how well do I know my solution?" and "Is my industry expertise an advantage, or is my weakness a disadvantage?" If the answer to either of these questions is not known, your fear of being outpositioned and blocked from the account by your competitors may come true.

Those who are feared are hated. You want the customer to realize that your competitors are riskier than you, uncaring, deceitful, and unable to fulfill the customer's fantasies. However, you need to understand what fantasies are. Most people think that fantasies have to be really big, like "One day I will be on the cover of *Time* magazine." In fact, fantasies can be very small. Some people think of fantasies only in a sexual context, when in reality most fantasies are quite mundane. Fantasies are just unfulfilled wishes. For example, you might wish to finish this book quickly. Until it's fulfilled, this wish is one of your many fantasies. You also might want to make $500,000 next year. That's a bigger, longer-term fantasy.

Customers' fantasies can be big or small, specific or general. For example, one customer might wish to leave work on time today in order to be home for an important family dinner. Another might wish to earn a promotion to the position of vice president. Someone else might desire to be left alone by the boss he dreads. Each of these fantasies has a different scope and duration.

Before a sales call starts, silently remind yourself that one of your objectives is to determine the fantasies of all the participants. Try to theorize what their short- and long-term fantasies are. Go ahead and make a deep psychological diagnosis about what is driving a person's fantasy. A person who wants a promotion to vice president to gain more power is quite different from someone who is seeking the promotion for personal validation or a bigger paycheck.

Remember, customers have many different types of fantasies and quite often they need help from vendors to fulfill them. Therefore, ignoring customers' fantasies is a big mistake. You must tap into them before your competitors do. However, customers will not usually broadcast their fantasies aloud. It's up to you to figure them out and convince the customers that only through your solution can their fantasies be realized.

When you have built relationships, demonstrated competence, and proved that you can fulfill fantasies, you will naturally dovetail with the internal politics of the decision-making process. Most importantly, using the indirect strategy of selling to the human nature of customers forces your competitors to use the direct strategy and sell based on the product itself. Because the indirect strategy is stronger, you put your competitors in a position of weakness.

Regardless of the complexity of your product or the sophistication of your customers, the final decision maker is always human nature. To validate this statement, all you have to do is think back to the deals you have lost when your product and price were best. You came in second place because you had third-rate relationships with customers. The only way to fight was lowering price in a frontal attack. From the standpoint of the human nature of sales, a competitor used his customer relationships to push you into the right-hand box in Figure 3.2. The customer had a negative perception of you and your solution. Or, in Napoleon's words, "In war, three-quarters turns on personal character and relations; the balance of manpower and materials counts only for the remaining quarter."[5] The same is true for sales.

STEP 3—ENLIST SPIES

How many times have you witnessed this scenario? A sales manager holds a forecast review session with his sales team. Since his main goal is to verify the accuracy of his forecast to his boss, he is solely focused on a here-and-now update. He only wants to know the odds of winning a deal and when the deal will close. The salesperson who doesn't fully answer these two questions is exiled from the meeting and told to get on the phone with the customer and find out the answers immediately.

Unfortunately, this exercise is a complete waste of time. Should the salesperson be lucky enough to track down the customer, the customer will not tell the salesperson the truth. Put yourself in the customer's position for a moment, being asked point-blank, "Where do we stand? Will we win? What do we need to do to win?" It's human nature to resist any direct approach. Remember the last time you were being pressured into doing something you didn't want to do? Whether the pressure came from a boss, spouse, child, or colleague, your natural response was to resist and push back. Therefore, the customer will not answer the questions directly or will provide misleading answers.

This entire sales-manager-and-salesperson drama could have been avoided by asking instead, "Who is our 'spy' and what does he have to say?" In other words, who acts as our eyes and ears when we are not around? Who is passing along secrets about what the other vendors are up to and telling us about the preferences of the various selection committee members? Who is telling us privileged and proprietary information that the other vendors aren't receiving?

The sales vernacular has many different terms for spies. They are also known as coaches, internal advocates, champions, and counselors. All of these advisers share a common characteristic. They have a selfish reason for wanting you or your company to win. This reason may range from the simple fact that they like you to the complicated nature of internal politics, where your solution helps them gain power, prestige, or authority.

Accurate information is the lifeblood of every deal, and the only way to get true information is through the use of a spy. Obviously, the more spies you have inside an account, the better the quality and quantity of information you will receive. The information received from these spies can be used to triangulate your position in an account and help determine your course of action.

Triangulation is a technique for comparing multiple data points to determine your true position. Determining your position in an account based on information from multiple sources is quite the opposite of dead reckoning, where you have only one source of information in an account. Being at the mercy of a single person is a risky position to be in. What if your spy is wrong?

Spies can be either weak or strong. Weak spies are observers who provide you information about the internal machinations of the selection process. They report the thoughts of the various selection team members and the movements of other vendors. Strong spies are not only observers, but they are also disseminators of information as well. Strong spies have a deeper, more personal connection to you than weak spies do. They're more akin to confidants than acquaintances. In fact, they are trusted friends who will courageously defend you and your solution when you are not around to do so yourself.

One of the most important aspects of spying is that it enables salespeople to truly understand the nature of an organization and who has the real power. Vested interests in a project go far beyond the names and titles on an organization chart. According to Sun Tzu, one of the spies' most vital missions is to gain a complete understanding of how the people are organized around the objective you are trying to overtake: "Whether the object is to crush an army, storm a city, or to assassinate an individual, it is always necessary to begin by finding out the names of the attendants, the aides-de-camp, the doorkeepers, and the sentries of the general in command. Our spies must be commissioned to ascertain these."[6] You must have a spy to win a deal. Without one, you will never know the true nature of the organization.

STEP 4—UNDERSTAND HOW THE OBJECTIVE IS ORGANIZED

It is vitally important to understand how your objective is organized. For example, Tien Tan sent spies to study the layout of the Yen camp and devised his strategy of attack based on this information. Most certainly, Tien Tan knew where the officers were quartered, the number of men in each of the various units of the Yen army, and where they slept.

He made the decision to use oxen in his attack based on the organization of the Yen camp. He had the oxen's horns equipped with sharp blades, their bodies painted, and their tails greased. When their tails were lit on fire, they furiously dashed from holes in the city walls made at precise locations and stampeded into the Yen camp. The havoc and destruction the oxen caused created a diversion that enabled Tien Tan's warriors to sneak into the positions where they could best launch an attack.

If you are involved in selling an enterprise solution, you already know the importance of understanding the inner workings of the various departments within a company. Your product might be purchased by the information technology department and used by accounting and manufacturing. It might be selected by accounting and used by marketing, research and development, and other functional areas of the organization. Or it could be selected by sales and bought by the purchasing department. Almost every purchase decision requires multiple departments to become involved. Therefore, it's critical to map out the interrelationships of the departments within an organization.

As a consultant, I have performed win-loss sales analysis studies for a variety of companies in many different industries. To complete these studies, I conducted blind surveys of the executives, departmental managers, and low-level evaluators who had selected or rejected the product from the company for which I was completing the study.

While the purpose of these studies was to improve the sales force's effectiveness, interesting patterns of organization behavior become apparent. These patterns supersede the standard hierarchical organization chart that salespeople have grown accustomed to studying.

Four models can be used to define the departmental interrelationships that influence a company's buying behavior: departments are either consolidators, consulters, responders, or bureaucrats. However, before we analyze each type of department, we must first define some company roles.

There are two types of liaisons, or intermediaries, between departments. The first are business liaisons, whose official function is to ensure a department is working well and satisfies the needs of the other departments within the organization. Business liaisons are the intermediaries who translate business needs between departments. In larger companies, common business liaison titles are "business analyst," "project manager," "facilitator," and "technical consultant." In smaller companies, the role of liaison usually is filled by departmental managers.

In one sense, every department within a company is a customer of every other department. And every department has very sophisticated users of the services of other departments. For example, the sales department has sales operations staff members who depend on information from the finance department. The manufacturing department has technical personnel who use information from research and development.

The employees who fill these positions are called "power users." To accomplish their departmental roles, power users are required to have an intimate knowledge of their department as well as the other departments. Or they must use the systems, information, equipment, or resources from another department to complete their jobs. Typical power users might have titles that include "specialist," "technician," "support," "administrator," or "coordinator."

Roles in a company can be divided into three basic categories: product, management, and executive. The product category includes those individuals who work hands-on with your product. These people use vendors' products to create new products for their companies. For example, a telephone operator creates communication (product) by using telephone equipment provided by vendors. A security officer safeguards assets (product) by using surveillance equipment from vendors. People within the product category have titles that explain exactly what they do, such as "computer programmer," "buyer," "mechanic," and "receptionist."

Individuals in the management category provide direction to one of the various departments of an organization. These departments are organized around functional areas of the company (finance, sales, marketing, manufacturing, and so on). Typically, people in this category may have "director," "manager," "supervisor," or "leader" in their titles.

In larger companies, the executive category is composed of people who have the word "president" or "chief" in their titles, such as the vice president, chief customer care officer, and chief technology officer. In smaller companies, the executive level may also include individuals with "director" or "manager" in their titles.

The four departmental types (consolidators, consulters, responders, and bureaucrats) have different orientations toward the operation of their departments. Most importantly, they buy products in different ways and for completely different purposes. It is important to understand that any department can be any type of buyer. For example, the finance department may be a consolidator at one company and a consulter at the next. Sometimes, the type of department may be associated with a specific business goal. For example, the finance department may be a consolidator when driving a project to complete Sarbanes-Oxley compliance and a responder when asked to assemble information for a sales department–driven project.

Consolidators

Consolidators are departments that seek to increase their power, authority, or control within their organization. To grow their sphere of influence, they launch grand initiatives, major company-wide projects that affect the operations of other departments.

The planning and creation of a grand initiative are at the direction of the department's executive leadership. This type of project does not percolate up from lower-level personnel through the chain of command; it is driven down from the top and out to the rest of the company.

Figure 3.3 illustrates a consolidator's flow of power. In this example, the vice president of the information technology department has decided to drive an initiative to move all applications and programs off the company's aging mainframe computers onto new, less expensive computer systems. After making this executive decision, he mandates that his direct managers fulfill his wishes. These direct reports assemble teams to plan the project and evaluate the vendors. The business liaisons who report back to the information technology department gather information from the various departments, schedule vendor demonstrations with departmental power users, and serve as intermediaries between the various departments during project implementation.

Notice that the boxes representing manufacturing and engineering are smaller than the information technology box and that the business liaisons box is larger than the power users boxes. This indicates who is more dominant and has superior power. The sizes of the boxes are different in the illustrations of the other types of departmental buyers.

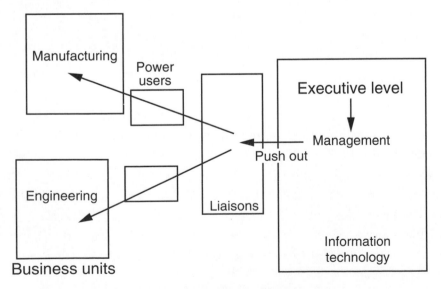

Figure 3.3   Consolidator Department Model

The underlying motivation behind grand initiatives like this one is always power, whether it's to gain more, consolidate it, or decrease that of other leaders and their departments within the organization. In this example, the information technology department is exercising its power over manufacturing and engineering. Sometimes a grand initiative is an executive-level coup, an internal revolution intended to change the way the company operates. Many times, it is a well-orchestrated conspiracy in the guise of a logical business project. Other times, it is an act of revenge against an intercompany archenemy.

Consolidators are typically a salesperson's dream because they have the propensity to make things happen. "Big-bang consolidators" tend to buy all the equipment and services they need to complete a grand initiative all at once. "Cautious consolidators," by contrast, purchase the products and services they need piecemeal, taking one small step at a time in order to prove their project's success.

Consulters

Consulters are departments that take on the characteristics and attributes of a consultant to their organization. They seek to understand the problems of other departments and offer recommendations on how those problems can be solved using their services.

They proactively share their proprietary knowledge and departmental expertise or offer unsolicited advice to other departments in an attempt to show how they can improve efficiency. Therefore, they are continually polling the other departments, seeking opportunities to promote their services, and pushing out their ideas, philosophies, and opinions. Liaisons are vitally important to consulters because they are gatherers and disseminators of information. As a result, liaisons have more power and influence with consulters than they do with consolidators.

Consulters are more prevalent in massive multibillion-dollar companies than in smaller organizations. They are less powerful than consolidators and achieve their desired outcomes through finesse rather than brute force. Since consulters are constantly seeking customers for their services, the power users are more likely to be within the consulter's department than in another business unit.

Figure 3.4 shows the information flow of a consulter department. In this example, the information technology department liaisons are constantly polling the business units for their needs and pushing out information they believe is beneficial.

For example, a liaison may seek out and meet with the vice president of sales, who expresses his dissatisfaction with the timeliness of the sales forecasting system. The liaison takes this information back to his department, and it traverses up the chain of command to where a decision is made to investigate new sales forecasting solutions. Conversely, a liaison may hear about an exciting new technology from the chief technology officer. The liaison schedules a meeting with the technology vendor to learn more. He

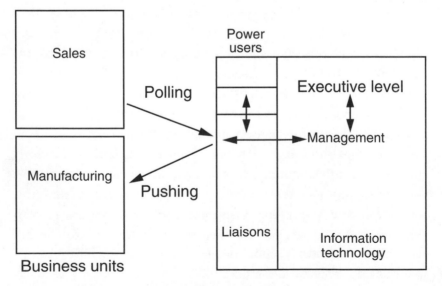

Figure 3.4   Consulter Department Model

then sets meetings with his constituents (power users of his department's services) in manufacturing to explain how the new technology may improve their operations.

Like a consultant hired on an hourly basis, consulters seek to continually validate their benefits and justify their existence to their customers. Selling to consulters differs from selling to consolidators because consulters enjoy the company of other consultants.

Responders

Responders are weak departments that operate under the direction of other departments. Whereas consolidators seek power and consulters seek to proliferate their services, responders are just trying to survive. Many times, responders are literally under attack from other departments that are unable to meet their objectives because of the responders' ineffectiveness. In some cases, the other departments have been disappointed by the responders' past blunders. As a result, responders tend to be treated disrespectfully and suffer from a lack of departmental esteem.

Figure 3.5 illustrates the power flow of a responder, in this case a marketing department. Once again, the sizes of the boxes reflect the departments' dominance and control. The power users can be very powerful in the responder model. In this example, the marketing department is the whipping boy of sales, constantly enduring that department's criticisms. Important power users within the sales organization complain to management that their needs aren't being met. In turn, senior executives dictate their needs to midlevel managers, who relay the message to marketing liaisons. In this instance, the liaisons' main goal is to run interference on behalf of their department, sorting out the most important requests while trying to maintain a semblance of departmental decorum. For issues of extreme importance and urgency, senior executives of a business unit will call their counterparts in marketing directly and tell them to get something done. The power is clearly on the business unit side.

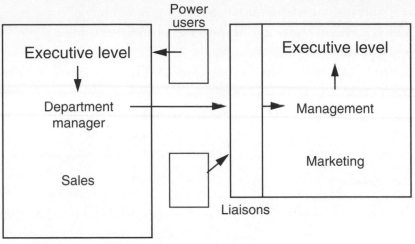

Figure 3.5   Responder Department Model

When selling to a responder, you must sell to the business unit as well as the responder, whereas with consulters and consolidators, your main sales effort should be directed inside their departments. For example, let's assume the sales department is complaining about lead generation (as always) and your company provides outbound telemarketing services. You need to make both the business unit (sales department) and the responder (marketing department) aware of your services.

Bureaucrats

The final category of departmental buyer is bureaucrats, faceless departments whose most important priority is to maintain the status quo through rules, regulations, and delaying tactics. The features of a bureaucrat department are secretiveness, a response system that reflexively rebuffs demands made upon the department, and administrative centralization around the departmental leader, the archbureaucrat.

The structured environment, similar to a military command-and-control environment, stamps out innovative thinking within lower levels of the department and hinders the free flow of information from other departments. Instead, the bureaucratic monarchy considers other departments outsiders and issues edicts that must be complied with for fear of consequences.

Figure 3.6 illustrates the shield that bureaucratic buyers erect around their department. In this example, the purchasing department dictates to the manufacturing department what products it will use. Meanwhile, the engineering department's recommendation is rejected, even though it is in the best interest of the company. One point to note is the lack of liaisons; the bureaucrat buyer is inwardly focused and less concerned about sensing the needs of other departments.

Every enterprise-wide sale involves consolidators, consulters,

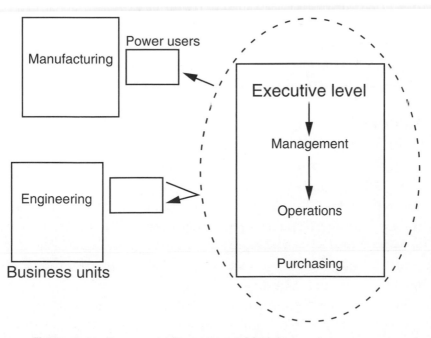

Figure 3.6   Bureaucrat Department Model

responders, and bureaucrats. You must determine a project's well-spring in order to know to whom and how to sell your solution. For example, at one company, every employee had to undergo ergonomics training on the proper way to use computers. Based on just this information, you might assume that the driver behind this company-wide initiative was the human resources department and that it was a consolidator. However, human resources was actually a consulter, working on this project at the direction of the finance department (the real consolidator). The finance department had instigated this project so that the company would qualify for reduced insurance premium rates.

Different Types of Value

Because executive leaders of consolidators, consulters, responders, and bureaucrats have different motivations, they have different perceptions of a product's true value. The perceived value of a product depends on the psychological, political, operational, and strategic value it provides the executive decision makers.

Customers spend far more time living with their decisions than they do making the decisions. Therefore, the decision to start a project or buy a particular product is usually made before the official decision-making process even begins. At the root of every decision is one of four psychological values or benefactions. As previously discussed, people buy products they believe will help them fulfill deep-seated psychological needs: satisfying the ego, being accepted as part of a group, avoiding pain, and ensuring survival. All the other outward appearances of a customer's decision-making process—the analysis, return on investment calculations, and other internal studies—are the means to achieving an overriding psychological goal. Therefore, the psychological value is most important when it comes to purchasing decisions.

The second most important value, political value, involves organizational power. Many people think that power is dependent upon title and that the way work gets done in organizations is through hierarchical authority. However, this is not usually the case. Power is the ability to influence the environment for your benefit and to get your way when it would be impossible otherwise. For example, while I have parental authority over my children, they have their own types of powers and associated strategies to get their way. Companies operate in much the same way.

Your product provides customers the opportunity to achieve political power. Your product may enable consolidators to increase their power, help consulters become indispensable to the company, allow responders to satisfy an internal power broker, or enable bureaucrats to maintain authority. Interdepartmental coordination always involves the use of power. Your product can make someone more powerful, or for those seeking power, it can provide much-needed visibility that enables them to be in contact with the company's power brokers.

The third most important value is operational value. People's success in an organization is dependent upon the success of their department's operations. Therefore, every department has inherent pressure to accomplish projects that successfully add operational value. The ways that operational value is determined are quite diverse. An ambitious consolidator might consider your product's operational value the ability to successfully complete its project. For a consulter, operational value might be that your product enables the department to proliferate its services throughout the company. Responders prize satisfying internal customers in other departments, and operational value to bureaucrats might be found in products that enable them to resist change. For example, a bureaucrat information technology department might add a new Internet interface to its existing mainframe rather than replace the entire system.

Strategic value, the fourth value, is based on the appearance of rationality and impartiality. However, customers do not seek information that will help them make an objective strategic decision; they amass information that helps them justify their preconceived ideas of strategic value. In other words, your product's strategic value comprises the reasons and arguments evaluators give to senior management and others in the company as to why the product should be purchased, regardless of whether the reasons are real or imagined. The seven types of strategic value enable customers to:

1. Gain a competitive advantage (increase market share, enter new markets, defeat competition).

2. Increase revenues.

3. Decrease costs.

4. Increase productivity and efficiency.

5. Improve customer satisfaction.

6. Improve quality.

7. Standardize operations (increase ease of business).

Consolidators will say that a purchase provides a competitive advantage or will enable them to increase revenues. Consulters might argue that it will save money in the long run. Responders will show how customer satisfaction will be improved, and bureaucrats will detail improvements in operational efficiency. Figure 3.7 summarizes how consolidators, consulters, responders, and bureaucrats view each of the four different types of value.

Messages to all types of buyer departments should be based on these four values. You must communicate to potential buyers that you can help solve critical department problems or help them become experts and an internal source of knowledge. For example, a company was planning an e-mail marketing campaign targeted at

	Consolidators	Consulters	Responders	Bureaucrats
Psychological value	Self-gratification	Physical well-being	Self-preservation	Pain avoidance
	Fulfill desire to achieve	Satisfy will to survive	Gain approval of others	Avoid painful change
Political value	Consolidate power	Become indispensible	Draft off the powerful	Maintain authority
Operational value	Enable the grand initiative	Proliferate service offerings through organization	Reactively accommodate internal customers	Do as little as possible
Strategic value	Gain competitive advantage	Improve quality	Improve customer satisfaction	Standardize operations
	Increase revenues	Decrease costs	Improve productivity and efficiency	Maintain ease of business

Figure 3.7   Different Types of Value Based on Type of Buyer

the automobile industry. The company sent me the following e-mail and asked for my opinion.

> Subject: Increase Profitability and Maintain Dealer
>   Partnership Loyalty!

> Dear Mr. Smith,

> My name is John Johnson from XYZ Corporation. We are the leader in providing solutions that help accelerate time to market and improve customer communications. We're helping customers such as Ford, Toyota, and Boeing automate their relationships with their distributors, dealers, and parts suppliers.

> In a recent strategic implementation, we were able to deliver Ford a robust solution that allowed them to communicate more effectively with their worldwide dealer distribution channel, drastically increasing customer service and loyalty.

XYZ Corporation can help you:

- Improve communications with critical partners.
- Speed time to market and increase dealer retention.
- Implement a "best practices" approach for all enterprise communications.

For a free evaluation of our robust solutions, please call or e-mail me at your earliest convenience.

Best regards,
John Johnson

What follows is my version of the same e-mail. While I didn't significantly change the main message, my goal was to tap into all the different types of customer values.

Subject: How Ford Maintains Its Critical Relationships

Dear Mark,

Q. How do Ford Motor Company, Toyota, and Honda maintain near-perfect dealer relationships?

A. XYZ Corporation has helped them automate and streamline all aspects of partner communications. As a result, they have increased revenues, accelerated time to market, and improved dealer communications.

For example, Ford distributes thousands of unique messages and memorandums to its worldwide dealer distribution channel on a daily basis. Ford has drastically reduced turnaround times while increasing customer service and loyalty using XYZ's solution.

For a free dealer communication analysis or to learn how we can improve and standardize relationships with all your important business partners, please call or e-mail me at your earliest convenience.

Thank you,
John Johnson

The most important aspect of this e-mail is not the points made of benefits; rather, it is the psychological impression it creates on the reader. In this regard, my goal was to invoke the Stockholm syndrome, a psychological phenomenon in which hostages develop a bond with their captors, named after an incident involving kidnapped bank employees in Stockholm. The most often cited example is newspaper heiress Patty Hearst, who helped rob banks with the radicals who kidnapped her.

When salespeople try to penetrate a new account, they are considered enemies, akin to bank robbers, so they are met with disdain and fear. Salespeople must turn negative resisters into positive accomplices. In this instance, I was trying to make the e-mail recipient become psychologically attached to the sender. A consolidator might envision starting a grand project like Ford's for his own personal gain. A consulter might want more information so he could impress others with his expertise. A responder might have been criticized about his dealer communications in the past and thought, "If it is good enough for Ford, it should work for me." Finally, a bureaucrat might be excited about standardizing all the various communications the company must send to its partners. The psychological storyline of the e-mail speaks to each type of departmental buyer.

STEP 5—GO AFTER THE LEADERS

The final step of the five steps to victory is to go after the leaders. Every sales cycle has several leaders in addition to yourself. The salespeople you are competing against are the leaders of their teams. Most importantly, a critical executive leader within the customer's company is ultimately responsible for making the buying decision. Knowing each of the leaders in an account is of paramount importance.

Sun Tzu said, "If you know the enemy and know yourself, you

need not fear the result of a hundred battles. If you know yourself but not the enemy, for every victory gained you will suffer a defeat. If you know neither the enemy nor yourself, you will succumb in every battle."[7] However, many salespeople don't spend a great deal of time thinking about their competitors. They think only of their actions and what they will do next. When they do think about the competition, it's in the general terms of the rival company, not the individual gladiator they must defeat.

The best way to defeat enemies is to take the time to place yourself in their exact positions. You must think like them in order to determine their strategies, priorities, and mental and emotional states. This is how General Patton outfoxed his archrival, Field Marshal Erwin Rommel, known as the "Desert Fox," in the deserts of North Africa. While the battles between these adversaries were intense, Rommel was actually defeated before they even began.

After serving in World War I, Rommel taught at military academies and published a book on strategy titled *Infantry Attacks*. Patton was a serious student of military history who read the memoirs of Napoleon Bonaparte and carefully analyzed Julius Caesar's battles. He was also the only World War II general who took his wartime library collection with him on the battlefield. Patton stayed up late many nights reading and rereading Rommel's book. As a result, he possessed the ultimate advantage: He could read his opponent's mind and anticipate his next move.

How well do you know your enemies? How much time do you spend studying their web sites, products, and marketing collateral? Do you take the time to perform an honest win-loss analysis after each engagement? Most salespeople argue that they simply don't have enough time for these types of activities. However, history repeats itself for those who don't learn from it. Even though Patton's dyslexia caused him to read far slower than average, he still found the time to study and read.

When I was a sales representative, I was frequently assigned to work at my company's booth at industry trade shows where my competition had booths as well. I always went out of my way to introduce myself to my counterparts. My teammates frowned on my socializing with the enemy and couldn't understand why I did it. However, I was on covert intelligence missions. I wanted to understand how competitors perceived us, learn their attitudes toward their own companies, and figure out the quality of people they employed.

When I walked up and introduced myself to them, some acted arrogant and others seemed embarrassed. Some would ramble on about how well their companies were doing, and others would hint that they were looking for new job opportunities. All the while, I was trying to profile my enemies and obtain vital information about how to compete against them.

The most important leader to go after in the entire sales process is the "bully with the juice." In *Heavy Hitter Selling* (Wiley, 2006), I described the universal law of sales, which is that every selection process has only one true leader, and this person single-handedly selects the winner. This person is known as the bully with the juice.

People who insist that things be done their way are called bullies. Bullies will get their way at any and all costs. *Bully* is not necessarily a negative term, nor does it mean that someone is physically intimidating. It is simply the description of people who will tenaciously fight for their cause. In the sales process, people are more likely to be bullies when they have an elevated status within an evaluation team. The status could be the result of their domain expertise or their title and the authority it commands.

Simply put, juice is charisma. But even this definition is too simple. People with juice are natural-born leaders. They have an aura that can motivate and instill confidence. That's juice. However, having juice does not mean that these people are the highest-ranking people involved in an evaluation. Instead, they are the ones who always seem to be on the winning side.

Only one member of the customer's evaluation team is the bully who has the juice. He imparts his own will on the selection process by single-handedly selecting the vendor and pushing the purchase through the procurement process. He can either finalize the purchase terms or instruct the procurement team on the terms that are considered acceptable. This is the leader you need to go after.

The bully with the juice has the ability to override the product selection made by other decision makers and even stop the procurement process. In the late stage of a deal, a bureaucrat from purchasing or the legal department might move into the position of the bully with the juice. Sometimes a battle is fought to find out who has more juice, the bureaucrat or the person who previously occupied the position of bully with the juice.

If your account doesn't have a bully with the juice, you should be prepared for no decision to be made. Conversely, if a bully with the juice does exist but you aren't able to identify the person, be prepared to lose the deal because you are in a position of extreme risk.

People will argue that some purchases are truly made by committee. While a committee does put more "fingerprints of accountability" on the product selection, behind every committee is a bully who has the juice. This person is responsible for creating the committee or is the person to whom the committee presents its recommendations.

Remember, you must always go after the leaders. The winning warrior is the first one who captures the heart and mind of the bully with the juice.

CONCLUSION

During World War II, the United States spent more money to develop the B-29 bomber than on the atomic bomb. The long-range bomber had four powerful engines and was capable of flying at 30,000 feet, safely above almost all antiaircraft fire. It was the perfect plane to fly across the vast stretches of the Pacific Ocean and drop bombs directly on Japan.

However, when first introduced to the Pacific theater, the plane was a near failure. The conventional bombs dropped at high altitudes encountered the newly discovered jet stream and widely missed their marks. As a result, the key military factories in Tokyo were able to continue producing weapons. Meanwhile, the number of planes lost during these daring daylight raids was mounting.

When General Curtis LeMay took command of the B-29 squadrons, he decided to completely change the strategy by which they were used. First, he studied reconnaissance photos of Tokyo to understand how the city was laid out. He recognized the density and proximity of the buildings to one another. His plan also took into account the materials (paper and wood) that comprised most of the buildings.

To the dismay of the bomber crews, he then had the B-29s stripped of all the defensive machine guns. The gunners who manned them were removed from the flights as well. The goal was to make the planes as light and fast as possible. He then equipped the planes with newly developed napalm incendiary bombs. But the most radical change in strategy was that the planes would fly at night at only five thousand feet. Upon hearing about the plan, the crews thought they were being sent on a suicide mission.

LeMay first used this new strategy on the industrial section of Tokyo. The factories in this section had survived numerous conventional bombing runs unscathed. The new strategy was not to bomb these factories directly from way above as in the past but to destroy them indirectly by setting the buildings around them on fire.

On March 10, 1945, 329 bombers took off for Tokyo and conducted the most destructive air raid in history. The firebombs burned 16 square miles of Tokyo, including all of its industrial center. Whereas the bomber losses were minimal, one hundred thousand civilians lost their lives.

A few days following the raid, Japan's leadership, the emperor and generals who commanded the country, toured the area of destruction. No doubt the bombings undermined their belief they could win the war. The emperor also began to worry that the citizens of Tokyo might revolt against him should the destruction continue.

LeMay's B-29s would go on to firebomb 63 other cities, killing nearly one million people. The attacks were both physical and mental warfare intended to break the spirit of the Japanese people. They set the tempo for the final months of the war, clearly showing the Japanese leadership and citizens how much the momentum had changed. In military terms, LeMay's new strategy, which was based on the five steps to victory, was a complete success.

For the sales warriors of the business world, the difference between being hailed as a hero or branded a failure hinges on winning. You must win. But in order to win, you must know the steps it takes to develop a winning strategy. Winning is everything in sales as it is in war.

PART TWO

Secrets of Persuasion

AFTER SALESPEOPLE have formulated their winning strategy, they use the second element of sales wisdom, persuasion, to turn skeptics into believers. Salespeople are paid to persuade. But what makes them persuasive? Is it their command of the facts and their ability to recite a litany of reasons why customers should buy? Could it be their charismatic presence and their natural ability to say the right words at the right time?

It takes more than logic and reason to change buyers' opinions. A personal connection must be established. Only through intense one-on-one conversations will skeptical prospects understand your point of view, appreciate your differences, and believe in you to the point where they become customers.

How can you get skeptics to come around to your way of thinking? Not only must you influence the customers' rational intellect with your business reasons, but you must project yourself into their subconscious. The hard and soft skills of persuasion can be learned by emulating successful practitioners, so in this part we will study three of the most persuasive communicators of all time.

CHAPTER 4

Real Persuasion

> Sky and earth will wear out; my words won't wear out.
> —JESUS CHRIST
> *The Message*

O ne early September morning, a hundred other airplane passengers and I were waiting on the runway for an unusually
long period after our plane's scheduled takeoff time. The travelers
were mainly businesspeople, and we were all in a hurry to reach our
destination and make critical meetings that lay ahead. As a veteran
road warrior who has flown millions of miles, I prepared myself for
the worst and thought the delay might be caused by mechanical or
weather problems.

Forty-five minutes later, the plane started to turn back to the
boarding gate, to the groans of everyone on board. Then the captain interrupted our complaints to inform us of the horrendous
acts of terrorism that had caused the nation's entire air space to be
shut down for the first time in aviation history on that day, September 11, 2001.

All the passengers were stunned and stared at one another in
momentary disbelief. As the vice president of sales, I instinctively
grabbed my cell phone and tried to find out where my salespeople
were. I worried most about our teams in New York, Boston, and
Washington, D.C. Later that day, after the unbelievable events had
unfolded, I sent the following e-mail to all the employees of my
company.

SUBJECT: NYC
  DATE: Tue, 11 Sep 2001
    TO: All
  FROM: Steve Martin

There is no adequate way to describe today's events. Thankfully, all our employees are accounted for. I happened to be waiting on the runway in an airplane when the captain solemnly broke the news to the passengers. It was a moment I will always remember. My prayer for today:

> We are pressed on every side by troubles, but we are not crushed and broken. We are perplexed, but we don't give up and quit. We get knocked down, but we get up and keep going.
>
> 2 Corinthians 4:8

Please take a moment and pray for the many, many people who are affected by this tragedy.

Steve

Thinking back about it now, I am surprised I sent that e-mail. In all my years in business, I had never seen any company communication that included any religious reference. It's just not considered politically correct in the business world. In one sense, it was risky to do personally as I was unsure how people would react. However, no more appropriate words could have been said at that moment.

The reaction to that e-mail completely surprised me. The responses came from believers of all religious faiths, and all the reactions were equally positive. Some thanked me and told me it was comforting. Even a professed atheist wrote me to tell me he considered the words "very appropriate." Everyone seemed to understand that my message was about the resilience of the human spirit and moving forward in the face of uncertainty, not about any particular theology.

I began to think how unfortunate it is that we can't talk about our respective religions in the workplace. Aside from the moral and spiritual lessons to be learned, the business world would benefit greatly from the practical information, wisdom, and common-sense advice that can be found in the Bible, Koran, and Torah and the teachings of Buddha and Confucius. Moreover, the words in each of these spiritual works not only are beautiful but serve as compelling examples of the persuasiveness of language.

Something else very profound happened to me that September day. I had spent the better part of my 20-year sales career on the road away from home. A typical workweek would find me traveling across the country to meet with customers and then back home again for the weekend. I can remember how I used to proudly show my elite-status frequent-flyer cards as a testament to my travel prowess.

When I wasn't away from home, I was a workaholic who kept long hours at the office. Even though I wasn't physically at the office on weekends, my mind was still consumed with business and, most importantly, the forecast. My career was my number one priority in life, and I even relocated my family far from our home in order to get ahead. After all, the move was really in their best interest, I rationalized to myself.

The events of that day made me stop and reevaluate my priorities. Actually, 9/11 *persuaded* me to change. It was a visceral event that penetrated my entire psyche and made me question my life's purpose. I kept thinking, *What if I had been on one of those planes?* A few weeks later I made a huge decision: I quit my job. I also did something I had never done before: I started to write my first book.

I share the preceding story with you for two reasons. First, persuasion requires a personal connection between people. People will naturally grow closer to you when they understand your motivations and identify with your situation. Second, the story also shows the role that human nature and emotions play in the decision-making process.

DECISION MAKING 101

How do people make decisions? Let's pick a topic that we have to make decisions about all the time—food. A recent Harris Poll found that 80 percent of Americans over the age of 25 are over-weight.[1] This figure has risen from 64 percent in 1990. The U.S. Surgeon General estimates that being overweight causes as many as four hundred thousand premature deaths each year and that the situation has reached epidemic proportions.[2] Health risk factors attributed to being overweight include high blood pressure, diabetes, heart disease, cancer, high blood cholesterol, stroke, gallbladder disease, asthma, and sleep apnea. Some people discriminate based on a person's weight. Overweight people may be paid less in the workplace and suffer more frequently from clinical depression. The facts are overwhelming, yet people continually decide to eat the wrong foods and overeat.

Here's another topic we constantly have to make decisions about—money. How much credit card debt do you have? The average American owes a total of $8,400 on eight different credit cards, and the credit on two of those cards is maxed out. Americans pay lenders $1,000 a year on average in finance charges.[3] A university professor recently said that credit card debt among college students poses a greater threat than alcohol or sexually transmitted diseases. Most distressing, *BusinessWeek* reported that for the first time in our country's history, total household debt (on credit cards, car loans, mortgages, and so on) topped 100 percent of disposable annual income in 2003.[4] In other words, we don't have enough money to pay our bills—we're broke! While business bankruptcy rates have fallen, personal bankruptcies are at an all-time high. The facts are overwhelming, yet people continually de-cide to overspend.

Based on these facts, everyone should maintain a healthy weight, and if we were completely rational decision makers, personal bankruptcies would be decreasing. However, it takes more than plain facts to change someone's mind, and our decisions are not made by logic alone.

Persuasion is not solely the recital of logical arguments or factual information to a listener. Instead, it is the process of projecting your entire set of beliefs and convictions onto another human being. It's not about getting others to acknowledge your arguments or agree with your business case; it's about making them internalize your message because they believe that's the only way to make real change happen. Ultimately, persuasion is the ability to tap into someone's emotions and reach the deeper subconscious decision maker within everyone, as September 11 did to me.

Who taught you how to become persuasive? You probably learned much of what you know by trial and error. Or you might have known a naturally persuasive coworker, friend, or colleague and tried to emulate your mentor's methods, honing your skills through informal and infrequent interactions.

You may have taken debate, public speaking, and communications classes while in school. However, they most likely focused on hard skills, such as the memorization and presentation of structured arguments. Anyone can recite facts, and two people can say the exact same words with entirely different results. Mastering the soft skills—understanding how to build rapport with skeptics, how people process and interpret information, and how to dovetail your ideas into a person's personal desires—is what ultimately makes someone influential.

To demonstrate these soft skills, we will use three linguistic role models: Ronald Reagan, Jesus Christ, and Buddha. We'll examine how they used language and communicated their ideas. We are not interested in their theology or political ideology. Rather, we want to understand how they motivated people to change their opinions and made believers of skeptics. We're most interested in the characteristics of communication these three persuasive people had in common.

- They spoke to each person individually. Persuasion isn't a one-size-fits-all proposition. It must be tailored to the individual.

- They spoke with compassion. More than empathizing with the listener, they understood the listener's passions.

- They spoke with congruence. They meant what they said and they said what they meant.

- They connected with the senses when they spoke. By engaging the listener's senses, they were able to touch the deep psychological drives that influence decision making.

- They told stories to illustrate their ideas. Buddha, Jesus, and Reagan were master storytellers and they cultivated this ability for good reason. Metaphors are the indirect approach of persuasion.

We'll spend the rest of the chapter walking through each of these characteristics in our attempt to become more persuasive ourselves.

SPEAK TO EACH PERSON INDIVIDUALLY

Let's start our investigation on the secrets of persuasion by examining one of my favorite stories from the teachings of Buddha.

> Once there was a man on a long journey who came to a river. He said to himself, "This side of the river is very difficult and dangerous to walk on, and the other side seems easier and safer, but how shall I get across?"

So he built a raft out of branches and reeds and safely crossed the river. Then he thought to himself: "This raft has been very useful to me in crossing the river; I will not abandon it to rot on the bank, but will carry it along with me." And thus he voluntarily assumed an unnecessary burden. Can this be called a wise man?

This parable teaches that even a good thing, when it becomes an unnecessary burden, should be thrown away; much more so if it is a bad thing. Buddha made the rule of his life to avoid useless and unnecessary discussions.[5]

The first time I read this story, I instantly thought of sales forecasting. Now I know you are thinking that Buddha never intended for this story to be about forecasting, so please allow me to explain.

At many companies, once an account is put on the forecast, it is virtually impossible to take it off. In many cases this is the salesperson's fault. If he has been working on the account for weeks or months and invested much time and effort, he simply can't drop the account (even though deep down he knows he has lost). This reminds me of the man who continues to carry the useless raft.

At other companies, sales management has created so much revenue pressure that it is impossible to take an account off the forecast. The salesperson who tries to do so will be subjected to the sales equivalent of the Spanish Inquisition by management. As a result, the forecast is filled with half-truths and lies. In these situations I invoke what I call "sales amnesty," whereby salespeople can clear out their forecasts and prune all the dead accounts without retribution.

What makes Buddha's story so profound is how it is interpreted individually by the receiver and that we can derive present-day meaning from a story thousands of years old. The concept is explained further in *The Teaching of Buddha*: "What Buddha preaches in His language, people receive and assimilate in their own language as if it were intended exclusively for them."[6] The first lesson about real persuasion is that it is based on this concept of personal interpretation. The term for this is "broadcast-unicast messaging."

What was your interpretation of the story? Maybe you thought about a habit you have that was once enjoyable but is now destructive or perhaps about a relationship that was initially beneficial but is now burdensome.

Now let's examine one of Christ's broadcast-unicast messages.

> What sorrows await you who are rich, for you have only your happiness now. What sorrows await you who are satisfied and prosperous now, for a time of awful hunger is before you. What sorrows await you who laugh carelessly, for your laughing will turn into mourning and sorrow.[7]

Although a message is broadcast to a group of people, each listener finds a unique meaning depending on his or her individual circumstances. People who consider themselves poor may transpose the warnings onto a wealthy person they know and rationalize that it is better to be spiritually rich than materially prosperous. Conversely, wealthy people may have felt a twinge of incrimination and performed a quick examination of their self-worth instead of their net worth. From a single passage, different listeners derive their own personal meanings.

We use many types and gradients of persuasion, depending on whom we are presenting our arguments to. For example, persuading a child to eat peas is much different from persuading the board of directors to pass your resolution. When you have to make a big presentation to a room filled with all types of people from different areas of a customer company, structure your message using the broadcast-unicast technique. Your goal is to have each attendee take away his or her own personal message from your presentation. You want each person to have a positive feeling about your solution and how it will impact his or her role in the company.

SPEAK WITH COMPASSION

All salespeople know they should listen intently when a customer talks. However, when it's *their* turn to talk, many become like Shakespearian actors on center stage. They feel compelled to prove they know every line of their company's sales script. Long orations about your product will not win over the customer's heart, whereas speaking compassionately will. The three elements of compassionate persuasion are having empathy, understanding the listener's passions, and speaking with passion.

Buddha gave a great definition of empathy when he said, "Your suffering is my suffering and your happiness is my happiness."[8] Even though empathy is a core human emotion, not everyone is equally empathetic. Empathy is now thought to be a genetic trait determined by your DNA makeup. It is estimated that 15 to 20 percent of the U.S. population are so-called empaths, people born with the trait of high sensitivity.[9]

If you are not a natural empath, the pause-to-check method can help improve your sensitivity. After every sentence you say during a sales call, pause for a moment and check with your audience. Specifically, check for nuances in their facial expressions and how they are holding their bodies. Do you think they are more engaged or less engaged? Why? It's okay to stop and ask, "Is everyone still with me?" or "Did I confuse anybody?"

Empathizing with customers is usually not enough to persuade them to buy. The "passion" part of compassion is what can swing a decision your way. All buyers have secret desires they want to fulfill. Buddha said, "People grasp at things for their own imagined convenience and comfort; they grasp at wealth and treasure and honors."[10] Understanding these desires and showing how your solution can help customers achieve them is at the heart of persuasion. (Refer to Chapter 3 for a detailed discussion of psychological, political, operational, and strategic values that drive executive decision makers.)

The other persuasive aspect of passion is how salespeople speak to customers. Your honest enthusiasm for your company and its products will permeate your customers' minds. The most persuasive salespeople are passionate about the company they work for and what they do for a living. However, their passion is not ostentatiously displayed like a cheerleader's pompoms. It is displayed in the confident way they demonstrate their product knowledge, the ease with which they talk about their company, and the cheerful disposition with which they approach their job.

SPEAK WITH CONGRUENCE

Congruence is more than truthful communication. It is speaking from the inside out. It is a genuine alignment between your internal beliefs and your spoken words.

Let's take a look at three statements from Ronald Reagan, Buddha, and Jesus Christ. What do they have in common?

Mr. Gorbachev, tear down this wall![11]

Ronald Reagan had three pillars of disdain in his life: big government, taxes, and communism. Of the three, he despised communism the most. Reagan described communism as a form of insanity and a devious disease: "When a disease like communism hangs on as it has for a half century or more it's good, now and then, to be reminded of just how vicious it really is. Of course those who have the disease use all kinds of misleading terms to describe its symptoms and its effects."[12]

Ronald Reagan had been an ardent anticommunist his entire life. He didn't adopt his stance on communism after polling the voters for hot buttons like politicians do today. Nancy Reagan would later say, "All of his ideas were formulated before he became governor or certainly before president."[13] The man who said "I believe it is our pre-ordained destiny to show all of mankind that they, too, can be free without having to leave their native shore" was speaking directly from the heart.[14]

Reagan was simply saying what he truly believed. His words were congruent with who he was and were internalized as a part of the fiber of his being. In 1987 when he said those famous words at the Brandenburg Gate, the barrier between the people of East Berlin and West Berlin, he was speaking from the inside out.

> You must break the bonds of worldly passions and drive them away as you would a viper.[15]

Since skepticism is the typical reaction when someone tells you what to do, why would anyone follow Buddha's advice to break the bonds of worldly passions? The answer is credibility, and credibility is achieved through personal experience. Let's examine how Buddha's mind set was influenced by his experiences growing up.

For 20 years, his father, King Shuddhodan Gautama, and mother, Queen Maya, had unsuccessfully tried to have children. To their joy, a son was finally born to them and named Prince Siddhartha, which means "every wish fulfilled."[16] However, the happiness of the birth was short-lived because the queen died a few days later.

Losing his mother deeply affected the prince as he grew up. As the seven-year-old began his training in military arts, his mind focused on the suffering in life—how a bird carried off a worm and why a tree had a scar—according to *The Teaching of Buddha*. "For the following ten years the prince was immersed in a life of pleasure, but always his thoughts returned to the problem of suffering as he pensively tried to understand the true meaning of life. 'The luxuries of the palace, this healthy body, this rejoicing youth! What do they mean to me?' "[17]

His struggle to find meaning drove him to turn his back on a life of luxury and leave the castle. He spent the next six years in the forest practicing asceticism. With austere self-discipline and denial of all worldly pleasures, the man who would have become a rich and powerful king owned nothing and relied on the generosity of others to stay alive. He spent the next 45 years of his life preaching and persuading people to follow his simple way of life. His life was a direct example of the words he spoke. Buddha's words were congruent with his being.

I am the way, the truth, and the life.[18]

Typically, people just don't describe themselves using the words "I am" in the manner Jesus Christ did when he said, "I am the way, the truth, and the life." Most of us speak such words as "I am" only when we are asked the question, What do you do for a living? People's responses to that question will tell you a lot about them. People who are proud of their profession will answer with specificity: "I am a doctor" or "I am the president of a division of a Fortune 500 company." For others, the answer may reveal their life's purpose: "I am the mother of my children." Meanwhile, the insecure or embarrassed will avoid a direct answer and might say, "I work for a retail company" or "I'm in the entertainment industry."

We are very unlikely to use the phrase "I am" publicly, and on the occasions when we must, we try not to expose too much personal information. For example, we don't rattle off everything we do well in life and risk being called a braggart, nor do we list all our struggles since we don't want to be considered a complainer. Therefore, we edit ourselves to conform to society's standards.

We are much more likely to use the phrase "I am" when we talk to ourselves internally, and that's usually in the context of our shortcomings. Personally, I am more likely to tell myself that I am a failure at something than I am great at something. However, Jesus Christ's usage of "I am" was a positive, expressive, intimate, and profound definition of who he was. This provides another important lesson about congruence. Congruence is based on a positive perception of yourself.

"I am" is also a binary statement, a yes-or-no proposition. Either you are a doctor, a president, or a mother or you're not. Most interestingly, this concept also extends to customers when they meet you. They can sense your congruence and whether or not you are who you say you are. Surprisingly, their decision about whether you have congruence happens very early in a sales call. Without congruence, you are considered untrustworthy, and everything you say will be met with skepticism.

Congruence is not only corresponding words and thoughts that corroborate each other, it is also the alignment of the *entire* body in delivering the message. For instance, do you think Jesus would have made his statement in a monotone voice or with a lackadaisical demeanor? No. I suspect he delivered those words passionately.

In the same way, Ronald Reagan didn't plead or suggest that Russian general secretary Mikhail Gorbachev tear down the Berlin Wall. He demanded it be removed. Here's the full context of what he said: "Come here to this gate! Mr. Gorbachev, open this gate! Mr. Gorbachev, tear down this wall!"[19] Those powerful words changed history.

Congruence is at the heart of persuasion. But how can you improve your congruence? First, you should know your product inside out. This alone will build your credibility. I am constantly amazed at how little average salespeople know about the products they sell. You can't believe in what you don't understand. You need to understand your company: its history, what makes it unique, and its future direction. You need to understand the customers you sell to and the problems they face, and you need to understand yourself. Why would someone buy from you? What are your strengths and weaknesses? Which accounts do you belong in and why?

Finally, the words you say to yourself are the most important words you use all day. Do you continually question yourself, or do you say positive reinforcements throughout the day? Do you tell yourself "It's just a job," or are you excited about what you do for a living? Your internal mantra, whether good or bad, will be conveyed to customers. Reagan never questioned his beliefs, Buddha did not doubt his purpose, and Jesus Christ knew exactly who he was.

CONNECT WITH THE SENSES

The business world has established standards of behavior that people are expected to adhere to. Businesspeople are supposed to hide their true feelings as much as possible and speak in nonpersonal, systematic terms. For example, instead of saying "it seems to me," they should say "the data suggests." Unfortunately, many salespeople believe they are being persuasive when they speak in the same way. However, this is a far cry from the way Jesus, Buddha, and Reagan spoke.

Why did Jesus say "It is easier for a camel to go through the eye of a needle than a rich person to enter the Kingdom of Heaven"[20] when he could have said "Rich people face more significant challenges to get to Heaven"? Why would Buddha say "The human mind, in its never-ending changes, is like the flowing water of a river or the burning flame of a candle; like an ape it is forever jumping about"[21] when he could have said "The human mind is restless"? Why would Reagan say "I've never been able to understand why a Republican contributor is a 'fat cat' and a Democratic contributor of the same amount of money is a 'public-spirited philanthropist' "[22] when he could have said "Republican contributors are unfairly judged"?

Engaging the senses is a fundamental part of persuasion. Picturing a camel trying to get through the eye of needle imparts a powerful image. Jumping from the topic of a river to a candle to an ape actually demonstrates the mind's impetuousness. Wordplay between "fat cat" and "philanthropist" not only keeps the audience engaged but highlights the unfairness of the comparison.

Our senses invoke our emotions and our emotions impact our senses. We cry when we see someone else crying and we grimace for others in pain. When we're angry, our field of vision narrows and our hearing intensifies. At the root of our emotions are deep personal drives, which in turn affect our emotions and our senses. The old saying "Our feelings are connected to our faces and our faces are connected to our feelings" is true. Figure 4.1 shows the extent of these interrelationships.

Let's apply this model to the salesperson's world. Following are the first few sentences from four different real estate ads. As you read through them, pick the house you would be most interested in buying. Try to notice how each ad engages the senses differently and creates a slightly different emotion. Also, try to determine

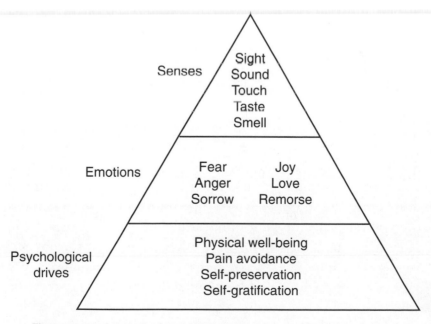

Figure 4.1 Interrelationships between Senses, Emotions, and Psychological Drives

whether the ad is geared to physical well-being (maintaining our mental, emotional, and physical health); pain (eliminating or avoiding it); self-preservation (gaining the approval of others); or self-gratification (serving the ego).

> This spectacular contemporary residence sets the standard for the neighborhood. Like the beautiful and stylish architecture treasures that inspired its design, the estate is something new and significant.
>
> Imagine the pleasure of living in a brand-new home with breathtaking ocean, white-water, and coastline views. Take a refreshing dip in the dramatic pool. This is an idyllic neighborhood where evening strolls beckon.
>
> The perfect family home! The home is situated on a cul-de-sac, very private, safe, and a fabulous backyard with large grassy areas.
>
> Large home, three bedrooms, three baths, large master bedroom, kitchen with upgraded cabinets, pool, easy access to freeway.[23]

Which one did you prefer? The first ad is based on self-gratification and appealing to the ego. Did you relax a little as you read the second ad? It's based on physical and emotional well-being. The third ad is very interesting because your interpretation depends on your home situation. Maybe you want to sequester your family from the world's dangers. If so, physical well-being is important. If you want to be the patriarch who provides the perfect lifestyle for your family, then self-preservation could be a driver. Perhaps your family situation isn't all that great. You might believe a new home would improve your circumstances and take away the pain.

What did you think about the last ad? That ad could actually describe any one of the other homes. Even though it provides more basic facts about the home, it is far less compelling.

Like the author of the last ad, some salespeople feel compelled to give only the facts about their products. They recite their products' features and functions with all the emotion and excitement of the alphabet. They mistakenly think that a deadpan delivery makes them seem more credible, when it only makes their solutions blend in with all the others the customer is evaluating.

Sales is not just the left-brain activity of presenting a sequence of objective, logical reasons to buy. Sales is also a right-brain, intuitive activity.

Paint a picture for customers of how your product will be used. Explain how excited they will be to tell others how it has helped them. Help them see themselves using it, and make them feel comfortable that in the end they will be happy and all their dreams will be realized.

TELL STORIES TO ILLUSTRATE COMPLEX IDEAS

Buddha, Jesus, and Reagan were all master storytellers. In fact, Jesus and Buddha taught almost exclusively telling stories, parables, and anecdotes. These stories were actually metaphors used to impart important life lessons, introduce complex new ideas, and persuade people to follow them. Jesus explained, "That's why I tell stories: to create readiness, to nudge people toward receptive insight. In their present state they can stare till doomsday and not see it, listen till they're blue in the face and not get it."[24]

Using metaphors is a nonthreatening way to make skeptics more receptive to your message. The three different types of metaphors are educational, personal, and action-based. Educational metaphors are analogies that help explain new concepts using common terms or everyday situations. When you make a drawing of your product's architecture to show the customer how it operates, you're using an educational metaphor. The story you tell about how one of your customers is successfully using your product is an example of a personal metaphor. Action-based metaphors use physical movement or action to communicate additional meaning and highlight important concepts. For example, a product demonstration is actually an action-based metaphor for how a customer can use your product. Site visits and reference calls are action-based metaphors intended to get customers to simulate product ownership.

As we review some of the stories that Jesus and Buddha told, try to determine whether each story is an educational, personal, or action-based metaphor. Note the differences in why the stories are used and how they are structured. Also, try to decipher each story's meaning from the standpoint of a salesperson. What lesson does this impart to you?

Here's the story of the king and the elephant from *The Teaching of Buddha*.

> Once upon a time a king gathered some blind men about an elephant and asked them to tell him what an elephant was like. The first man felt the tusk and said an elephant was like a giant carrot; another happened to touch an ear and said it was like a big fan; another touched its trunk and said it was a pestle; still another, who happened to feel its leg, said it was like a mortar; and another, who grasped its tail, said it was like a rope. Not one of them was able to tell the king the elephant's real form.[25]

One interpretation of this educational metaphor is that you blindly make decisions when you do not have all the information.

A limited perspective will cause you to draw the wrong conclusion. From a sales standpoint, when you rely on one person for all your information about a deal, you are seeing only the tusk, trunk, or tail. You need multiple perspectives to get the true picture of what's going on inside the account.

Here's another story paraphrased from *The Teaching of Buddha.*

> When the moon sets, people say the moon has disappeared; and when the moon rises, they say that the moon has appeared. In fact, the moon neither goes nor comes but shines continually in the sky. People call one phase of the moon a full moon, and they call another a crescent moon; in reality, the moon is always perfectly round, neither waxing nor waning. The moon appears everywhere, over a crowded city, a sleepy village, a mountain, a river. It is seen in the depths of a pond, in a jug of water, in a drop of dew hanging on a leaf. To men the moon seems to change, but the moon does not change. Buddha is like the moon in following people of this world in their changing circumstances, manifesting various appearances; but His Essence does not change.[26]

This story is interesting because it is both a personal metaphor and an educational metaphor. It also shows how you can combine and layer the different types of metaphors for maximum effectiveness. Looking at the moon is the personal part of the metaphor. It is something everyone is very familiar with. The metaphor of the moon is then used to educate readers about the complex nature of Buddha.

Did you notice the imagery used in this metaphor and picture the various phases of the moon, the sleepy village, or the moon rising over a mountain? This is an important point about metaphors:

you must draw the listener into them. For example, if you are describing how a customer is successfully using your product, not only does the story need to be interesting, but it must also cause prospective customers to place themselves within the story. You want them to imagine themselves as your customers.

From a sales standpoint, this metaphor can be interpreted in several different ways. One interpretation is that sometimes the obvious is misleading. In the same way as we see the crescent moon, we may see a deal coming our way, but we could be completely wrong. The metaphor also points out the nebulousness of words. Customers may say they are looking to solve a particular problem or need a specific feature but use words that don't accurately reflect what they really want. It's our job to find out what they truly need. It's also a story about the nature of the truth. An observer sees the moon in many different shapes, but the truth is that it is always round. All the salespeople working on a deal believe they can win it. However, only one winner will emerge. Your goal is to look past your misperceptions and truthfully determine whether you can win the deal.

Whereas the previous metaphor was a conceptual comparison of the moon to Buddha, the following is a narrative story from the New Testament about Jesus Christ. The story starts as Jesus is traveling to the village of Galilee.

> He had to go through the city of Samaria on the way. Jesus, tired from the long walk, sat wearily beside a well about noontime. Soon a Samaritan woman came to draw water, and Jesus said to her, "Please give me a drink." The woman was surprised, for Jews refuse to have anything to do with Samaritans. She said to Jesus, "You are a Jew, and I am a Samaritan woman. Why are you asking me for a drink?"
>
> Jesus replied, "If you only knew the gift God has for you and who I am, you would ask me, and I would give you living water."

"But sir, you don't have a rope or bucket," she said, "and this is a very deep well. Where would you get this living water?"

Jesus replied, "People soon become thirsty again after drinking this water. But the water I give them takes away thirst altogether. It becomes a perpetual spring within them, giving them eternal life."

"Please, sir," the woman said, "give me some of that water! Then I'll never be thirsty again and I won't have to come here and haul water."

"Go and get your husband," Jesus told her.

"I don't have a husband," the woman replied.

"You're right! You don't have a husband—for you have had five husbands and you aren't even married to the man you are living with now."

The woman left her water jar beside the well and went to the village and told everyone, "Come and meet a man who told me everything I did!" So the people came streaming to the village to see him.[27]

As opposed to the "once upon a time" fairy tale beginning of the elephant metaphor, this action-based metaphor is a narration of events that sets a different mood for the reader. The metaphor reveals many lessons that are applicable to sales, such as how to establish rapport with strangers and win over new customers.

As Jesus traveled from town to town, he needed to be aware of the local customs just as salespeople who journey from customer to customer today must adapt their behavior to each customer's particular environment. In those days men rarely spoke to women publicly and a Jew would not consider talking to a Samaritan. Regardless, Jesus was there to create new relationships, and by saying "Please give me a drink" he set the tone of their interaction.

Selling is a process as well as a specific result. The most important part of the sales process is getting customers to help your cause. The salesperson must take the initiative of starting the process and must set the tone of the conversation. Christ started the discussion by saying a very powerful word: "please."

The sales process continues as both parties try to understand each other's needs. Relationships are created when people share the same activities or when they are motivated to achieve the same goals. Goals can be defined as very personal prioritized desires (benefactions) where a personal benefit is gained from taking an action to satisfy the desire. The Samaritan woman wanted some of the "living water" Jesus spoke of so she would never be thirsty again. But what did Jesus want?

Although Jesus started the conversation by asking for a drink, I am not convinced that's all he really wanted. His benefaction was to preach to the people of her town. Now, he could have accomplished this in a different way, such as by yelling at the top of his voice for everyone to gather around (a direct strategy). But how would the people in this town have reacted to a stranger? Rather, he needed to find someone to arrange the meeting for him who was a part of the community, understood its ways, and knew its people.

Information plays an important role in every sales cycle, and its value depends on its accuracy, timeliness, and confidentiality. Jesus knew some personal information about the woman. How do you get privileged intelligence about a deal you're working on? By building a deep relationship with someone within the customer's organization. As we discussed in Chapter 1, obtaining privileged information through the use of spies is a fundamental principle of the indirect strategy.

A special relationship developed between the Samaritan woman and Jesus. As a result, she ran through town exhorting others to come hear him talk (an indirect strategy). Instead of thinking he was a potential enemy passing through town, the townspeople gathered around him to hear his message.

Ronald Reagan also used metaphors but in an entirely different way. He loved to tell funny stories and jokes. He told them for a purpose that went way beyond just getting a laugh. He used them to make political statements. Speaking about Vietnam War protesters he said, "The last bunch of pickets were carrying signs that said 'Make love, not war.' The only trouble was they didn't look capable of doing either."[28] Describing politics he said, "Politics is supposed to be the second-oldest profession. I have come to realize that it bears a very close resemblance to the first."[29]

Self-deprecating jokes, in which he poked fun at himself, actually helped improve his image as an average American: "I have left orders to be awakened at any time in case of national emergency, even if I'm in a cabinet meeting."[30] To disarm his critics he said, "Republicans believe every day is the Fourth of July, but the Democrats believe every day is April fifteenth."[31] One of his favorite jokes was the pony joke about twin boys who were five or six years old.

Worried that the boys had developed extreme personalities—one was a total pessimist, the other a total optimist—their parents took them to see a psychiatrist. First the psychiatrist treated the pessimist. Trying to brighten his outlook, the psychiatrist took him to a room piled to the ceiling with brand-new toys. But instead of yelping with delight, the little boy burst into tears. "What's the matter?" the psychiatrist asked, baffled. "Don't you want to play with any of the toys?" "Yes," the little boy bawled, "but if I did I'd only break them." Next the psychiatrist treated the optimist. Trying to dampen his outlook, the psychiatrist took him to a room piled to the ceiling with horse manure. But instead of wrinkling his nose in disgust, the optimist emitted just the yelp of delight the psychiatrist had been hoping to hear from his brother, the pessimist. Then he clambered to the top of the pile, dropped to his knees, and began gleefully digging out scoop after scoop with his bare hands. "What do you think you're doing?" the psychiatrist asked, just as baffled by the optimist as he had been by the pessimist. "With all this manure," the little boy replied, beaming, "there must be a pony in here somewhere!"[32]

Reagan told this joke so often that whenever something would go wrong at the White House, a member of his staff would be sure to say, "There must be a pony in here somewhere."

Like a seasoned salesperson, Reagan had a knack for making pithy comebacks that rendered his opponents' political body blows ineffective, thus allowing him to escape his position on the ropes. In the 1984 presidential debate, age figured to be a big issue since challenger Walter Mondale was 17 years younger than Reagan. To counteract potential criticism that the oldest man ever to serve as president was too old for the job, Reagan said, "I will not make age an issue of this campaign. I am not going to exploit, for political purposes, my opponent's youth and inexperience."[33]

Every salesperson should follow Reagan's lead and use humor during sales calls. It shows you don't take yourself too seriously. If you tell jokes, the punch line should always be self-deprecating and at your expense. Observational humor about common experiences such as children, traffic, or taxes is a safe area, too. When people laugh, at some level they must agree with you. Humor helps build rapport and lower the defenses between buyers and sellers. Remember, everyone is somewhat nervous during a sales call, and humor lightens the mood and helps everyone relax.

CONCLUSION

What is your company's greatest sales weapon? Is it the patents, products, or brand name? Technologies will come and go as new products are continually introduced into the market. (I doubt you have recently bought any record albums, a typewriter, or a Ford Pinto.) And while we tend to think of a company's brand as unique, it is only as valuable as the integrity of its people. Enron, WorldCom, and Tyco were once very respected company names.

In reality, the most important weapon in your arsenal is the words you speak to customers. Let's summarize the major points from this chapter, using the words of Buddha, Jesus Christ, and Ronald Reagan.

Reciting your product's long list of features, functions, and business benefits will not persuade the customer to buy. Persuasion is the ability to gain the willing obedience of others, as exemplified in this story from *The Teaching of Buddha*:

> Once there was wealthy man whose house caught fire. The man was away from home and when he came back, he found that his children were so absorbed in play, they had not noticed the fire and were still inside the house. The father screamed, "Get out! Get out! Come out of the house! Hurry!" But the children did not heed him. The anxious father shouted again. "Children, I have some wonderful toys here; come out of the house and get them!" Heeding his cry this time, the children ran out of the burning house.[34]

Using stories, parables, and other metaphors is a powerful, indirect method of persuading customers to buy. When Jesus Christ's disciples asked him why he always told stories, he explained, "To those who are open to my teaching, more understanding will be given, and they will have an abundance of knowledge. But to those who are not listening, even what they have will be taken away from them. That is why I tell these stories, because people see what I do, but they don't really see. They hear what I say, but don't really hear, and they don't understand."[35]

Finally, one of your greatest persuasive weapons is your sense of humor. A dog had been brought into the Oval Office, and the unruly canine was running around while President Reagan continued to do his work. Reagan's deputy chief of staff walked in and said, "Mr. President, if you don't get that dog out of here he's going to pee on your desk," to which Reagan replied, "Why not, everybody else does."[36] In the end, a quick wit is the salesperson's most valuable asset.

CHAPTER 5

Meeting of the Minds

> In the sky there is no east and west; people create the
> distinctions out of their own minds and then believe them
> to be true.
>
> —BUDDHA
> *The Teaching of Buddha*

I still vividly remember my driver education class from way back in high school. The instructor made us watch movies on the dangers of unsafe driving. These extremely graphic films had titles like *Red Asphalt*, and their gruesome crash footage terrified all of us teenage watchers. One movie showed an accident scene that involved a trucker who was forced to stop short, which caused his load of steel to slide forward through the cab. Twenty-five years later, I always give truckers plenty of room on the road because that image is still etched in my mind.

What images are etched in your mind? Your mind is unique. It is completely different from that of any of the other six billion people on the planet. It contains a historical record of your existence and one-of-a-kind thoughts that are individual to you. It has been shaped by your surroundings: where you grew up, where you went to school, and the jobs you have held throughout your career. Your attitude toward life has been influenced by your parents, siblings, friends, lovers, spouses, and enemies. The mentors in your life have influenced your moral compass, spirituality, standards, and beliefs. Meanwhile, the combination of your diverse personal traits, ranging from your extroversion to your assertiveness and self-discipline, causes your mind to act in certain ways that are particular to you.

When two people strike up a conversation, they believe that they are speaking a common language. However, the language they use is not truly universal. The source of all language is the mind, and since everyone's mind is so distinct, people actually talk in their own dialects. Therefore, if we want to communicate persuasively and learn how to make lasting impressions, we need to learn to speak different dialects. The process starts by understanding how the mind processes language.

Be aware that no one truly knows how the mind works. Although neuroscientists have named the parts of the brain and know their overall function, the three-pound pale gray organ that has a texture similar that of pâté remains a mystery. Even today's scientists using all of their sophisticated equipment cannot explain the origins of faith, hope, and love.

Most of the recent advances in understanding the inner workings of the mind have come from three different sources. The study of brain-damaged people has yielded information about how the various regions of the brain control the body. For example, Wernicke's area, located to the rear of the brain, is essential for language. People who suffer damage to this area can understand language but their speech does not make sense. They are still able to say individual words coherently, but they speak gibberish and their sentences don't mean anything.

Brain scans and neuroimaging techniques such as positron emission tomography (PET) and functional magnetic resonance imaging (FMRI) make it possible to observe human brains at work. They reveal changes in activity of the various brain regions depending on physiological activities. For example, while a person is seeing, hearing, smelling, tasting, or touching something, certain areas of the brain light up on the scan.

Finally, and most importantly for salespeople, is information gleaned from individual and group experiments. For example, researchers conducting a group study measured finger ratios of the participants and then asked them to complete a questionnaire measuring aggression. They found that shorter second-to-fourth-finger ratios predicted a person's proneness to physical aggression in men but not in women. This information can be used to theoretically predict a man's aggressive tendencies.

This type of testing is in many ways equivalent to what salespeople do every day. We go out into the world and try to interpret and understand the inner workings of our customers' minds based on shreds of information in order to predict future behavior. Salespeople could accurately be described as "mental investigators." (How would you like that title on your business card?)

Let's say you went on eight customer calls last week and met with groups ranging from 2 to 10 people, for a total of 50 people. What percentage of the people did you connect with? In other words, how many did you feel truly liked you, believed in your message, and wanted to see you again? Was it 20, 50, or 70 percent? Most likely, the percentage was lower than half and probably just a small fraction. The reason for this is that you had to connect with each person individually and each was in a group setting. You met with 50 people with 50 differently wired minds.

Let's examine the concept of connecting with individual minds through a discussion about recent U.S. presidents.

CONNECTING WITH MINDS

Why was Ronald Reagan called "the Great Communicator"? Some say it was his eloquence, some say his likability, and others say his acting ability. I would suggest that it was his ability to naturally connect with people. And this same ability, used in a slightly different way, enabled George W. Bush to defeat John Kerry in the 2004 presidential election. But how do people connect?

We connect with people through the words we speak, the way in which we say them, and the congruence of the words to our demeanor. However, the words we use are complex three-dimensional objects that don't mean the same thing to everyone. Let's do a word association exercise. For each of the following words, what is the first thought that comes to mind?

Dog
Cat
Sports
Church
Marriage

If you have a dog, you probably thought of your dog. A picture of your dog may have come to mind, and you may have said your dog's name to yourself. If you dislike dogs, you probably wondered how anyone could like those drooling, unruly beasts, while conversely, the word *cat* might have evoked positive feelings. The word *sports* may have caused you to think about the sport you played in school because words are anchored to our memories. The word *church* could elicit many different responses, ranging from a sense of purpose to resistance to authority, depending on your orientation. Meanwhile, marriage is to some a blessing; to others, a dream; and to the unlucky, a nightmare. So the word *marriage* is likely to evoke your feelings based on your experience.

All of these words have something in common. In order to be understood, they must be interpreted into something meaningful: familiar thoughts and terms. This process occurs in three steps: determining the lexical meaning of a word, translating the word into personal meaning, and finally, forming a psychological impression determined by how the word is cataloged.

Lexical Dictionary: Did I Understand What Was Said?

The first step is comprehension, checking whether the word can be found in the personal dictionary you keep inside your mind. Your lexical dictionary determines your word comprehension. The average person's dictionary contains about 50,000 words. However, all words are not equally persuasive. General words such as *performance*, *reliability*, and *quality* by themselves are not influential. Operator words, words that improve the persuasiveness of general words, must be added to influence a customer's mind. Adding "nine hundred pages per hour" to define performance adds a comparison-point meaning. Adding "one hundred thousand hours mean time between failures" to specify reliability makes the word more convincing. Believability is improved when "lifetime guaranteed replacement" is associated with quality.

New words are continually being added to your lexical dictionary. For example, you may not know the meaning of the word *amorphous*. However, you can derive its meaning when you hear it used in a sentence such as "The customers gave a vague and amorphous answer when asked when they would make a decision." Operator words work in much the same way. They allow you to introduce new concepts to customers by deduction. For example, when you say, "Our multiprocessor architecture results in performance that is three times faster than the competition's," the customer deduces that multiprocessor is advantageous.

Sometimes the terms your marketing department believes are so important and persuasive actually detract from your credibility. I have probably reviewed more than one hundred corporate PowerPoint presentations in the past year alone. Not only do they all look the same, they all use the same general words to describe their company's unique advantages. Open your corporate presentation and see how many of these terms and phrases you can find.

World leader	Increase revenues	Scalable
Market leader	Reduce costs	Manageable
Best in class	Competitive advantage	Reliable
Best of breed	Greater productivity	Powerful
Cost effective	Improve customer	Easy to use
End-to-end	satisfaction	Dynamic
solution	Better visibility	

These words have been so overused that they actually have a negative impact or no impact at all. So while you're thinking you are saying something profound to customers, they're rolling their eyes and saying to themselves, "Here we go again!"

Personal Meaning: How Do I Interpret the Words Personally?

After your lexical dictionary has defined a word, personal meaning is associated with it. For example, your lexical definition of the word *children* might be "kids between 2 and 12." In your mind, children are not teenagers or babies. Your mind then tries to derive personal meaning from the word *children*. If you have children, you might immediately think of your son, daughter, or all of your children. You might have thought of a child playing or even a schoolroom. Another level of personal interpretation occurs.

Word Catalog: How Do the Words Affect Me?

The deepest level of meaning occurs inside the mind's word catalog. This is where the word is decomposed into its base object and associated with complex psychological meaning. While your lexical dictionary defines the basic meaning of words, your word catalog links that meaning to your feelings from past experiences.

Your word catalog has been profoundly influenced by your life's experiences, which are unique to you. These experiences, both good and bad, have shaped your perception of the world. Through your senses, you are constantly adding to your cumulative knowledge of how your world functions. As you accumulate new experiences, they are edited and influenced by your history. As a result, it is accurate to say that every person functions in his or her own unique world. Your world is your own personal reality. You use your word catalog to classify your experiences and describe your world to others. For example, the word *childhood* can evoke either positive emotions or bad memories, depending on how you cataloged your childhood experiences.

Through language, we represent our thoughts and experiences. We use words to represent the sensory experiences of sight, sound, touch, smell, and taste. The map we use to describe and interpret an experience is based on one of three word catalogs—visual, auditory, and kinesthetic. "Visual" refers to pictures and imagery, "auditory" to sounds, and "kinesthetic" to touch, taste, smell, and internal feelings.

Most people use one word catalog more frequently than the others. This word catalog has become their default, or primary, mode of communication. You can identify people's primary word catalog by listening to the adjectives, adverbs, and nouns they use in conversation.

Customers whose primary word catalog is based on sight will describe their experiences in visual terms. They are likely to say, "I see what you mean," "Looks good to me," or "Show me how it works." Customers with a primary word catalog based on sound will say, "Sounds great," "Talk to you later," or "Tell me how it works." People with a primary word catalog based on feelings might say, "Feels right to me," "We'll touch base later," or "I can't get a handle on how it works."

Some people are left-handed and some are right-handed. The dominant hand you use was not your conscious choice. Your brain was wired to use that hand. In addition, over time you have grown comfortable and proficient in using it more than the other.

Similarly, people have a dominant (primary) word catalog. They also have a weaker secondary catalog and, finally, a recessive catalog. People process information with their word catalogs using pictures, words, or feelings according to the strength of each catalog.

People do not use one word catalog exclusively. Instead, they use all three catalogs in different increments and priorities. For example, a person might say visual words 60 percent of the time, kinesthetic words 25 percent of the time, and only 15 percent auditory words when speaking. And the strength of each system and the order in which the systems are used can profoundly impact a person's ability to persuade.

Now let's return to the topic of the 2004 presidential election and analyze the word catalogs of John Kerry and George Bush.

WHY GEORGE BUSH WON THE 2004 PRESIDENTIAL ELECTION

The words you speak are not always the most important aspect of persuading someone to believe in you. For example, after Richard Nixon debated John Kennedy during the 1960 presidential election, radio listeners thought Nixon won, while television viewers preferred Kennedy.

While the decision to choose a president seems to be complex, it is actually quite simple. In fact, most people make up their minds about who they are going to vote for decades ahead of time, depending on whether they were raised in a Republican or a Democratic household. The common thinking in U.S. politics is that 40 percent of the voters are Republicans and 40 percent are Democrats; they'll always vote for their party's ticket. The remaining 20 percent of swing voters decide the election. Interestingly, the percentage of people who were undecided remained the same throughout the entire 2004 election. Therefore, pundits surmised that the candidate who won over the most swing voters would win the presidency.

The American Psychological Association released an interesting study that sheds light on how undecided voters decide. The study classifies U.S. presidents into eight different groups: Dominators, Introverts, Good Guys, Innocents, Actors, Maintainers, Philosophers, and Extroverts. In some cases, a president was placed in more than one group. The Dominators are Richard Nixon, Andrew Johnson, Lyndon Johnson, Andrew Jackson, James Polk, Theodore Roosevelt, and Chester Arthur. The Introverts are John Adams, John Quincy Adams, Richard Nixon, Herbert Hoover, Calvin Coolidge, James Buchanan, Woodrow Wilson, and Benjamin Harrison. The Good Guys are Rutherford Hayes, Zachary Taylor, Dwight Eisenhower, John Tyler, Millard Fillmore, Grover Cleveland, Gerald Ford, and George Washington. The Innocents are William Taft, Warren Harding, and Ulysses Grant. The Actors are Ronald Reagan, Warren Harding, William Henry Harrison, Bill Clinton, and Franklin Pierce. The Maintainers are William McKinley, George H. W. Bush, Gerald Ford, and Harry Truman. The Philosophers are James Garfield, Abraham Lincoln, Thomas Jefferson, James Madison, Jimmy Carter, and Rutherford Hayes. And the Extroverts are Franklin Roosevelt, John Kennedy, Bill Clinton, Theodore Roosevelt, Ronald Reagan, William Henry Harrison, Warren Harding, Andrew Jackson, and Lyndon Johnson.[1]

It's far easier to place George W. Bush into one of these categories than to place John Kerry. The Texan easily fits into the Good Guys category and could possibly be placed in the Extroverts group. Meanwhile, it's not clear what category the senator from Massachusetts belongs in. Whether selecting a president to lead the country or a salesperson to do business with, people will choose the person they associate with best, the person whom they can readily categorize into a familiar type of relationship.

What the candidates said also helped voters identify with them, and we can learn a lot about the nature of persuasion by studying the 2004 presidential campaign debates. John Kerry was a prizewinning debater in high school and class orator at Yale University and had spent the prior 20 years honing his skills arguing on the Senate floor. It's not surprising that he won all the debates. It also isn't surprising that the debates did not swing the presidency his way because the battle was between the supposed good guy and the good debater (another lesson for salespeople).

But here's where it gets interesting. Bush and Kerry have quite different word catalog wirings, and it seems this played a role in the election. Based on my observations, the respective strengths of their kinesthetic, auditory, and visual word catalogs are shown in Figure 5.1.

While Bush is a primary Kinesthetic, Kerry is a primary Auditory. A primary Auditory has an ear for words and is a master of language. However, when an Auditory does not have a strong kinesthetic word catalog, he will use analytical, unemotional terms and tend to speak in repetitious patterns. The most common pattern of a primary Auditory is speaking in a monotonic voice.

This helps explain the continual criticisms about Kerry during the election campaign: his delivery was stiff, he didn't show emotion, and he didn't know when to stop talking. While he had deep knowledge of the issues and could masterfully pontificate about policies, he couldn't connect with the people whose votes he needed to swing the election his way. I believe the best speech he gave was actually his concession speech. He would be president today if he had spoken like that on the campaign trail.

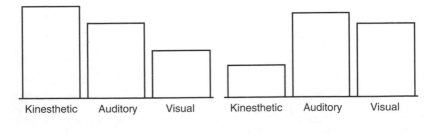

George Bush   **John Kerry**

Figure 5.1   Word Catalog Strengths of Bush and Kerry

Primary Kinesthetics have an intrinsic communication advantage over primary Auditories because they are always in touch with their own feelings and are sensitive to the feelings of others. While the words they say may not be as well thought out or intellectual, the way in which they speak comes across as genuine. Strong Kinesthetics tend to be more dramatic in their speech patterns and inflections. Unlike Auditories, with their Morse code speech patterns, Kinesthetics feel the words they are speaking. As a result, their tone of voice tends to be lower and they insert pauses and voice inflections. This is because they are constantly validating and comparing their feelings with what they are hearing and saying.

Bush's campaign staff strived to show Bush as a regular guy. Their strategy was to capitalize on his natural strengths to tap into the swing voters' feelings. As contrary as this sounds, people make even the most rational decisions based ultimately upon their emotions. Prior to the election, a *USA Today* article made these comments:

> Like any popular contestant on a reality show, Bush conveys the sense of an ordinary guy suddenly forced into unnatural, extraordinary circumstances—particularly after 9/11. His durable popularity rents on the fact that he hasn't puffed himself up as the great anything. In the spirit of populist television, he understands that the public wants likeability more than lordliness, the feeling of a decent, reliable fellow from next door rather than a superhuman candidate for Rushmore. He's the Good Neighbor President.[2]

Kerry's vice presidential running mate, John Edwards, said that one of the main lessons he learned from the 2004 election was that presidential elections "are not issue-driven"; rather, you must "show people who you are."[3] In the end, Bush had the natural communication advantage of likability. And if likability can win the presidency, it certainly can help you win more deals.

BALANCED COMMUNICATORS

During recent times, we have had two presidents who were extraordinary communicators. Presidents Ronald Reagan and Bill Clinton were both prolific speakers with unique abilities to persuade. However, what did "the Great Communicator" and "the Great Empathizer," as each was named by the media, really have in common?

When the relative strengths of their word catalogs are analyzed, we find very similar patterns. More importantly, their word catalogs are extremely balanced and of the same relative strength. None is far stronger than the others, as in the case of Bush and Kerry. Basically, the men were wired nearly equally, as Figure 5.2 shows.

It seems that balanced communication is a key attribute of effective persuasion. Balanced communicators create better rapport. They don't limit themselves by speaking exclusively from a single word catalog. They connect with Kinesthetics, Auditories, and Visuals equally. Therefore, a balanced speaker naturally reaches a broader audience. My best estimate is that out of ten businesspeople, four will be primary Visuals, four will be primary Auditories, and two will be primary Kinesthetics.

It's important to note that true word catalog usage can be verified only from natural conversation. The study of Clinton's

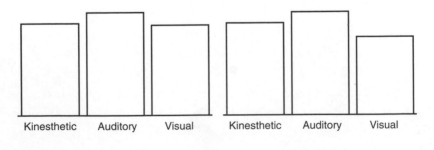

Figure 5.2   Word Catalog Strengths of Reagan and Clinton

and Reagan's wiring included debates, press conferences, and personal writings as opposed to speeches written by professional speechwriters.

I have also analyzed Jesus Christ's quotes from several different translations of the Bible. I counted the number of kinesthetic words he used—words such as *ache, breathe, caress, catch, crawl, feel, grab, hard, heart, heavy, sense, smell, smile, smooth, spit, taste, touch,* and *weigh.* Then I tallied auditory words, such as *ask, assert, banter, berate, boast, cajole, call, denounce, discuss, giggle, loud, plead, promise, shout, speak, tell,* and *yell.* Finally, visual words were added up, such as *bleak, blight, blind, bright, brilliant, clear, cloudy, disappear, fade, gaze, glance, glare, illuminate, light, look, shine, stare,* and *watch.*

The results were the same regardless of translation. When all the kinesthetic, auditory, and visual words were added up, about one-third were kinesthetic, one-third auditory, and the remaining third visual. In fact, the percentages of the visual, auditory, and kinesthetic words were always within just a few points of each other.

This data helps validate that persuasion and balanced communication work hand in hand. However, it's not only what you say but also how you say it that makes it convincing. This is because the subconscious mind connects to another dimension of language. And this deeper meaning of language plays an important role in decision making.

THE SUBCONSCIOUS DECISION MAKER

To further understand the impact of the subconscious mind on decision making, let's examine a fictitious case study of Bob, a college-educated professional. Successful in his career, he has risen to the rank of vice president at a division of a Fortune 500 company. Bob is a smart businessman who possesses sound business practices and the acumen to get to the top of the corporate ladder.

Let's say Bob is facing two very important decisions. The first decision involves making a multimillion-dollar purchase to upgrade some equipment of the division he runs. The second decision involves proposing marriage to Maggie, his girlfriend of nine months. Bob approaches each of these decisions in a very different way.

For the business decision, he first conducts an in-depth study of the inefficiencies of his current infrastructure. Next, he presents his findings from an internal rate-of-return study for replacing the old equipment with state-of-the-art machinery to the senior management team of the parent company. Then he performs a detailed analysis of the various equipment vendors and makes a final selection.

Getting married is one of life's most important decisions. Bob has fallen in love with Maggie. He feels good being with her, thinks about her often, and looks forward to their time together. She has the qualities he admires, and when compared to girlfriends of the past, she is the best. Bob decides he will ask her to marry him.

However, as Bob moves forward in his decision-making process with regard to the equipment purchase, an unexpected change in Bob's thought process occurs. The subconscious mind, the self-regulating system designed to prevent us from making unwise choices, is on vigilant watch. It drives Bob to perform a gut check of the rational, logical information regarding the equipment purchase. Beyond the facts and figures, does the decision feel right? He second-guesses himself and asks whether the move will help or hurt his career.

Conversely, the emotional high associated with the idea of marriage is tempered by reality. He now evaluates Maggie's little habits that he once thought were cute with a more rational eye. He studies other aspects of their relationship with equal intensity. Figure 5.3 illustrates the changing nature of the decision-making process.

Buddha best described this phenomenon in terms of two kinds of worldly passions: "The first is the passion for analysis and discussion by which people become confused in judgment. The second is the passion for emotional experience by which people's values become confused."[4] We've all worked accounts where, after studying every aspect of your product and your competitor's product, customers went into "analysis paralysis." They had so much information that they couldn't make a decision. At the opposite end of the spectrum are customers who change their minds on a moment-by-moment basis. You might be winning one moment and losing the next. Overwhelmed with information, the conscious mind vacillates from one extreme to the other.

At this point the subconscious mind takes an active role in decision making. One of its main responsibilities is protection. Much

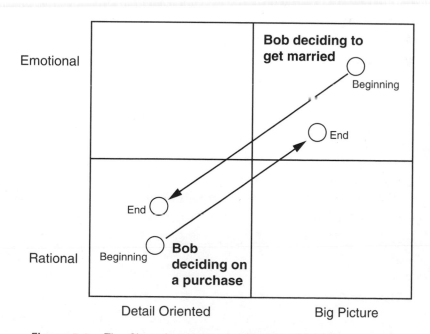

Figure 5.3   The Changing Nature of Decision Making

like a guardian angel, it's on the lookout for perilous situations and possible circumstances that might endanger the person physically and mentally. To perform this task, it assumes a third-person observation role and acts as a separate entity, even though it resides deep inside the individual. It guides a decision maker from the emotional to the logical and vice versa. Therefore, different types of persuasion are needed, depending on the type of decision that is being made and the stage of the decision process.

THE DIFFERENT TYPES OF PERSUASION

Twenty-four hundred years ago, Aristotle described the three elements needed to move an audience: pathos, logos, and ethos—the emotional appeal, the intellectual appeal, and the speaker's character and charismatic appeal. These classifications are just as applicable today, with one qualification. Logos is the direct approach to persuasion. Pathos and ethos are indirect persuasion approaches. In today's marketplace, where little difference exists between products, the indirect approach employing pathos and ethos plays a more important role in persuading customers to buy.

Logos: The Intellectual Appeal

All competent salespeople can recite their products' features, benefits, and specifications. Their companies have trained them on the business reasons to select their products, identified processes to educate customers, and established procedures to determine customers' technical requirements.

Since most salespeople are well versed on the logic of selling, it doesn't make sense to reiterate here what you already know. Instead, let's emphasize some steps you can take to make an intellectual appeal more compelling.

- Provide independent confirmation of your facts wherever possible.

- Provide quotes from authorities (customers, analysts, and the press).

- Quantify beneficial claims with specific numbers.

- Use real-world examples, which are more powerful than hypothetical statements.

- Arrange your arguments from strongest to weakest.

- Keep it simple. Remember Occam's razor: the simpler explanation is always preferred.

- Be prepared for contradictory facts from other vendors, and have factual responses ready.

- Quantify results from adverse consequences (for example, loss of revenue due to equipment downtime).

- Present the extremes to make the other options look worse than they really are.

- Use alliteration—repetition of the same letter or sound at the beginning of adjacent words—so that concepts are more easily remembered (for example, durability and dependability).

- Use the rule of three: whenever you make a claim, support it with three different facts.

- Create your own euphemisms that reflect the importance of your product or a particular feature. For example, a rubber band could be called a "multipurpose business instrument."

- Understand that it is all right to draw big conclusions from small statistics. Sometimes the biggest points can be made from the smallest samples.

- Brighten up the facts with interesting graphics that represent them pictorially.

- Become a storyteller, not a human dictionary. Use metaphors to explain concepts. Instead of saying "A poll showed customers prefer us three to one," say "Harris Poll surveyed four thousand buyers from across the country and found that three thousand, or 75 percent, thought our solution was far superior."

Logical arguments alone, no matter how well you present them, will not change skeptics into believers. Finessing customers to change their opinions requires an emotional appeal to their human nature.

Pathos: The Emotional Appeal

Most salespeople equate the emotional appeal to pleading with customers for their business. However, pathos is far more complex. It is creating a favorable disposition in potential customers through an emotional or psychological appeal while casting your competition in an unfavorable light.

In Chapter 3, we discussed the two most important aspects of the emotional appeal: the different benefactions that drive buyers and the importance of personal fantasies to win the hearts and minds of customers. The third critical piece of the emotional appeal is the buyers' reactions, the coping mechanisms they use when facing the stressful situation of selecting between salespeople. Coping mechanisms are psychological and behavioral strategies people use to manage stress and threatening situations.

It's interesting to watch people cope during an argument. During the heat of battle, people will say something about the other person that really describes themselves. In one hallway argument, a manager yelled, "You are always using your title to get what you want!" The funny part was that he was the CEO of the company, the person with the highest ranking in the company, who always used his title and the authority it commanded to get his way.

Similarly, sometimes what customers say about you really applies to them. They'll say your price is too high when, in reality, they couldn't afford it in the first place. They will say your solution is technically inferior when they don't need all the functionality or don't have the wherewithal to implement it.

Customers will not only say what they don't mean but mean what they don't say. When you are meeting face-to-face with someone, human nature dictates that the other person will avoid confronting or disappointing you. Perhaps the best way to explain this is through a personal story. My teenage daughter recently started dating. The first fellow she went steady with was a nice boy whom I really liked. Since I had befriended him, I was actually disappointed when they broke up. The next boyfriend I didn't care for at all, and I told my daughter so on several occasions (which only hurt our relationship). Thankfully, they broke up a short while later. From both of these experiences, I learned a valuable lesson: I couldn't become emotionally involved in my daughter's choice of a boyfriend. I had to keep my distance in order to protect my own feelings and those of my daughter.

Customers act in a very similar way. They like some salespeople and dislike others. Therefore, they instinctively try to keep the conversations with everybody at a business level in order to protect themselves. This is the most prevalent coping mechanism buyers use to deal with salespeople. Here's a short list of some other common coping mechanisms buyers use.

- *Attack*. Customers may categorize all salespeople as unethical evildoers and therefore attack you because you're part of the group. Do not take this attack personally. For example, some customers may continually refer to you derogatorily as a "vendor" or tell you that they cannot believe you since all salespeople lie.

- *Avoidance.* Some customers will seek to avoid people and situations that cause distress. Confronting customers who use this coping mechanism causes them to avoid you all the more. For example, a customer may recite standard party-line answers when you ask probing questions.

- *Compensation.* Customers will make up for a weakness in one area by overemphasizing a strength in another. For example, a business-oriented senior executive who can't follow the technical conversation his subordinates are having with the salesperson may blurt out that he is in charge of the selection.

- *Intellectualization.* Customers will avoid showing any emotion and focus instead on facts and logic. They rebuff your attempts to start a personal, nonbusiness conversation.

- *Passive-aggressiveness.* One of the worst predicaments for any salesperson is when a customer projects a friendly demeanor but is secretly plotting against you—for instance, the smiling customer who continually attempts to placate you with platitudes about your product.

- *Rationalization.* Customers will use logical reasons in an illogical way to publicly validate their emotional favorite. For example, they will explain that they are eliminating your company from their search because it does not have product support in Japan, although they don't have any operations in Japan.

- *Reaction formation.* Some customers will take a polar opposite position to everything you say. They simply don't want to buy from you. For example, when you explain why a particular feature is so important to all your other customers, they explain how it wouldn't help them, even though it would.

- *Trivialization*. Customers will trivialize a favored vendor's major deficiency while maximizing the minor shortcomings of the other vendors.

We naturally assume that customers will react in one of two ways to our pitch: They'll like it or they won't. However, customer behavior is far more complex. Customers use coping mechanisms to deal with the stress of being on the receiving end of someone asking for their business.

I'd like to make one final comment about pathos, the emotional appeal. In its lowest form, it is akin to begging. And in some circumstances, begging the customer for help is completely appropriate. For instance, you have a right to plead with a long-term customer to make a purchase in this quarter as opposed to the next one if you've helped that customer in the past. You're simply asking for a favor in return. There's also a time and place for pleading in new deals. I remember begging a low-level contact to help me set up a meeting with his boss's boss, telling him my manager was going to kill me if I didn't set up the meeting. This is also a sure way to find out whether you really have a coach in the account.

Ethos: Character and the Charismatic Appeal

The foundations of ethos are wisdom, virtue, and goodwill. When salespeople share their experience and opinions with customers, the wisdom of age and seniority are advantages. To show virtue, salespeople will follow customers' explicit and implicit instructions on how they should behave during the sales cycle. As an act of goodwill, salespeople will donate their time and their company's resources to an account, even though it is not fully known whether they are going to win.

All salespeople are trying to earn the customer's trust. They'll lend a sympathetic ear and try to become a trusted adviser. To prove they're dependable, they'll follow through on their commitments. They'll demonstrate their responsiveness and show they are active helpers. To show integrity, they'll speak the truth. For example, a friend of mine who runs a landscape business was asked to provide an estimate for trimming trees at a business center. He provided the customer with a quote for 28 trees. The customer called him and told him that there were 34 trees on the property. My friend responded that only 28 needed trimming. The customer awarded him the business on the spot because all of the other quotes were for 34 trees.

Customers have an entirely different perception of your character than you may think. They actually think of you in familial terms and try to characterize your association with them based on their personal relationships. For example, a salesperson may be characterized as a friend by one customer and as an acquaintance by another. He could be a little brother to an older customer or a big brother to a younger one. The salesperson could be a father, lover, uncle, cousin, or even an enemy. Figure 5.4 shows the different permutations of relationships between customers and salespeople.

It is human nature for customers to categorize you into one of these relationship groups. Knowing whether you are a little brother or a friend, and when to act like a buddy or a mentor, plays an important role in the customer's determination of your character.

Ethos is charisma as well as character. In the world of sales, being charismatic does not mean you must have the eloquence of Ronald Reagan or the magnetism of Bill Clinton. The salesperson's definition of charisma is transparency, the ability to be exactly who you are and the propensity to be perfectly frank about it. In other words, what people see in you should be exactly what they get.

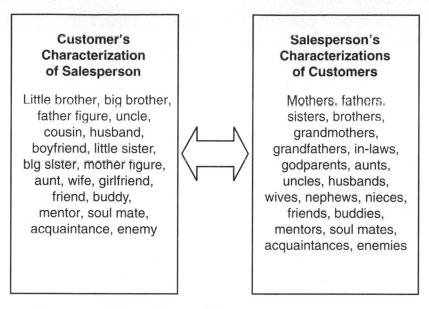

Figure 5.4   Different Types of Customer Relationships

Someone who has moved from a technical position into sales can be just as charismatic as a seasoned sales veteran. However, he has a different type of charisma. Instead of projecting a powerful presence, his deep-rooted technical understanding of his product draws customers to him. Some salespeople have such a lighthearted presence that customers will buy almost anything to keep them around—they're attracted to a humorous type of charisma. Others want to associate with someone better than themselves, a person who has a character trait they feel they lack. They may want to be around someone more outgoing, confident, charming, attractive, or worldly.

Many different flavors of charisma are presented in many different ways. How would you describe your type of charisma? In what types of accounts does your charisma work best, and with what kinds of people does it make you more persuasive?

THE PERSUASIVE CORPORATE SALES PRESENTATION

The old school of sales is based on the notion that the winners are the salespeople who build a better business case for selecting their product. I call this type of thinking the "Pavlovian sales model" because it is basically a stimulus-and-response way to sell. (Russian scientist Ivan Pavlov conditioned a dog to salivate whenever a dinner bell was rung.) Pavlovian corporate sales presentations are typically organized into six sections: my company, the products, how they work, the benefits, our customers, and call to action. Here's how these presentations are perceived by customers.

Vendor Stimulus
My company: "We're the biggest, the industry leader, the technology leader."
Customer Response
"The last vendor said the same thing."

Vendor Stimulus
The products: "State of the art, feature rich, advanced functionality."
Customer Response
"The last vendor said the same thing."

Vendor Stimulus
How they work: "Fast, flexible, easy to use, quick implementation."
Customer Response
"The last vendor said the same thing."

Vendor Stimulus
The benefits: "Reduce costs, make more money, improve efficiency."

Customer Response
"The last vendor said the same thing."

Vendor Stimulus
Our customers: "Successful well-known companies in the Fortune 1000."
Customer Response
"The last vendor said the same thing."

Vendor Stimulus
Call to action: "Give us your feedback and let's plan the next step together."
Customer Response
"The last vendor said the same thing."

The corporate sales presentation is a key moment in almost every deal. It is the pivotal event where all the vendors are asked to present their advantages and why they should be selected over everyone else. Usually, it is the deal's turning point. You might gain momentum and develop the personal relationships necessary to carry your solution across the finish line, or you could reach the apex of your involvement in the account. In the latter case, while most customers won't come right out and tell you that your presentation didn't fare well compared to the others, they will never treat you quite the same from that moment forward. *Buzz kill* is the term I use to describe a deal-breaking moment that is rarely overcome.

The creators of almost all of the hundreds of presentations I have reviewed over the past couple of years come not from sales but from marketing departments. Unfortunately, these people usually have had very little interaction with customers and no direct sales experience. They assume that customers think like they do and that the selection process is completely unbiased. Therefore, their presentation is a point-by-point list of reasons why a customer should select their product. Their list in turn is contradicted by the other presentations from the other vendors.

The folks in marketing aren't even aware that customers might not have the same word catalog wiring as they do. The most common mistake is made by those who are strong Auditories. Their presentations are slide after slide of boring bullet points of information, with very few graphics to break up the monotony. For Visuals in the audience, these presentations are "death by PowerPoint." Conversely, when a visual marketer creates a presentation, it has so many big-picture ideas and so much animation that only one person in the entire company can give the presentation effectively—its creator.

After sitting through so many presentations, I can honestly say that they all are basically the same. You could take slides from one company's presentation and insert them in another's and no one would notice. They are all fact-based infomercials that approach customers in a stimulus-response manner. In Pavolian terms, the vendors have rung the dinner bell so many times that the dog refuses to get off the couch to check his bowl.

It's not enough to say that to stand out you have to be different. Rather, you need a more sophisticated, indirect approach that differentiates your solution in the minds of customers. You can't *tell* customers you're unique, different, and one of a kind. You must *demonstrate* it to them, starting with the psychology of the corporate presentation.

The best corporate presentation takes into account the human nature of customers. The psychological theory of holistic interactionism includes the notion that behavior is not based solely on personality but ultimately is influenced by a person's situational interaction with the environment. For example, a gregarious extrovert is quiet and reserved while in a library. A self-conscious introvert might turn into a screaming maniac while rooting for his favorite team at a football game.

The holistic view of personal behavior takes into account the interaction between people (their thoughts, emotions, and person-alities) and the world that surrounds them at the same time. The situational nature of this theory helps explain why ethical business-people lie to salespeople. Some customers don't want to disappoint salespeople during the sales call so they tell the salespeople what they want to hear. Other customers seek to avoid face-to-face con-frontations so they keep their objections to themselves.

These are the circumstances that salespeople must work un-der, and corporate presentations involve the most complex environ-ment salespeople face during the entire sales cycle. The entire event is influenced by politics and peer pressure. Audience members have different agendas. Roles and titles do not clearly define power and responsibilities. Attendees not only have different reasons for at-tending the presentation but also have planned in advance to use the meeting to achieve different outcomes.

A successful corporate presentation depends on your under-standing the complete environment and the interactions between audience members. The optimum way to conduct a corporate presentation is through holistic interactionism, a person-centered approach that combines concrete thought processes (facts, features, and functions) with abstract thought processes (politics, environ-ment, feelings, and benefactions). It's not enough to explain how well known your company is and how your product works. The presentation goal must be to get customers to envision using the product so they drop their biases against your company and its so-lution, overlook intercompany politics that might work against you, and rally together around your cause.

The process of holistic interactionism starts with an investi-gation before the presentation to ascertain what the presentation environment will be like. Will you be interrogated Spanish In-quisition style or attend a Woodstock-like lovefest? While it is easy to find out who is attending and what their official titles are, under-standing the internal machinations of the customer's decision process requires a "spy." Only a spy can tell you who is for, against, or ambivalent to your solution. Only a spy can prepare you for the various objections that will be raised during the presentation, objections that could you throw you off track. Involving your spy in the creation of the presentation, finding out what points to cover and what to avoid, is critical. Previewing the presentation with your spy is ideal.

In the absence of a spy, use the upcoming meeting as an excuse to try to meet beforehand with those who will attend. This will help you get the lay of the land and determine the real reasons why they are evaluating different solutions.

Old-fashioned detective work is still vitally important. Fortunately, the Internet makes information more readily available than ever. Study every page of information on the customer's web site as though your life depended on it. Read the annual report, press releases, product information, and all financial documents. From these documents you will have to derive your strategic, operational, political, and psychological value statements (refer back to Chapter 3 for a refresher on these terms).

It's an imperfect world, and sometimes you don't have the luxury of prepresentation meetings. The customer might not allow them or you may not have enough time to schedule them. If this is the case, you will have to fall back on your intuition. Assimilate the information from your Internet study, adding it to your past experiences and knowledge of what does and doesn't work. Show the presentation to your colleagues to get their opinions as to where the holes are.

ORGANIZING THE PRESENTATION

The presentation itself should be divided into four sections. It should start with a pattern interruption, move on to customer metaphors, follow with the explanation and value section, and close with suggestions. This way of presenting is distinctly different from the Pavlovian-based presentations of all the other vendors. Let's examine each section of the presentation in detail.

Section I: The Pattern Interruption

Let's put ourselves in the position of the customer for a moment. We've sat through hundreds of different sales presentations through the years. Because these presentations have been based on marketing propaganda, one of our primary objectives is to delineate fact from fiction. Therefore, we are skeptical.

We've also met hundreds of salespeople during these presentations and have found most of them to be friendly, courteous, and professional. Each of them also wants to build a personal relationship with us. We can't let this happen. We aren't going to build friendships with everyone when we know only one person will be around for the long term. It's not practical or comfortable to do this. Therefore, we are reserved and on guard and we keep our distance.

Since you're the salesperson, the first goal of your presentation should be to perform a pattern interruption to break the customer's mode of thinking and stand out from the competition. The pattern interruption starts the process of building rapport, engages the audience, and provokes open-mindedness. It successfully sets the stage for the remainder of the presentation.

But what exactly is a pattern interruption? Let me explain with the following analogy. An Apple iPod can store thousands of songs. We have several iPods in my household, and I frequently listen to my teenage daughter's to check out the latest hits. As I thumb through her playlists, each song has just a few seconds to capture my attention. If the introduction isn't interesting, different, or exciting, I immediately move on to the next song. The term I use to describe this critical lead-in is *cowcatcher*.

Most people associate the term *cowcatcher* with the metal grill on the front of a locomotive. However, *cowcatcher* has an entirely different meaning in the entertainment industry. It's a show's opening moments in which the performers try to grab your attention and cause you to stop and look. The best corporate presentations start with a great cowcatcher.

A great cowcatcher engages the mind, appeals to the imagination, and helps the presenter gain credibility. For example, I worked at a company whose core technology was originally developed by the California Institute of Technology and funded by a grant from the National Aeronautics and Space Administration (NASA). Explaining the origins of the company—not with one simple slide with a few bullet points but using highlights of the project and its results set against the black backdrop of outer space with its millions of stars—was a great cowcatcher. We differentiated ourselves and gained instant credibility.

Another company I worked for was the top-rated NASDAQ stock for a period of five years. In fact, during one two-year time frame, $32,000 worth of this company's stock grew to be worth $1,000,000. I always opened my presentations with a chart of the stock price and some facts about the stock's appreciation. The customers would be more than intrigued; they were downright fascinated and eager to learn more. Many would buy my company's stock that very day!

Unfortunately, the first few slides of most corporate presentations have little panache. The obligatory introduction states some facts about the company's financial position, how long it has been in business, and its office locations. (The worst actually show pictures of the company's buildings as if this were something astounding.)

Section II: Customer Metaphors

One of the biggest problems that most salespeople have on sales calls is that they are too eager to tell the customer about their products. The same is true for a corporate presentation, and when this happens, the presentation does not build a story line that piques interest. Instead of launching into slides about the product line and technical aspects of the products, the second section of the corporate presentation should focus on customers.

Following the cowcatcher, you need a hook. Now that the listeners' interest is piqued, you need to hook them on why they should use your product. Your best hook is to tell them stories about your customers. Most corporate presentations include an obligatory slide that shows 20 or so logos of the major companies that use the salesperson's products. That's not what I am referring to here.

The second section should include six to eight slides of how specific customers are using the products, the operational results that have been improved, and the financial impact on the bottom line. In addition, it should include a quote from a customer whose name and title the audience can identify with psychologically. For example, include a quote from your customer's CFO when presenting to a financial department. Finally, this section should have some eye-catching graphics that tie the whole story together. These could be pictures of your product at work, the person who provided the quote, or an example of the end result.

The pertinence of the customer examples is very important. Presenting examples from companies that closely mirror the prospect's business or technical environment will make the statements more powerful. Presenting examples from companies that the prospects don't recognize will have less impact and, in reality, may actually hinder the argument because the prospect might think the product is not pervasive or popular.

At the lowest level of relevance, the companies you use as examples could be well-known organizations, such as Coca-Cola and Shell Oil. Certainly, these are companies that would be known by the customer. The level of relevance improves when the example companies are known for their past innovations, such as FedEx and

Intel, or are well respected for their quality and brand, such as Mercedes-Benz and Nordstrom. By providing examples of customers that have a dominant position in an unrelated business, the salesperson also receives implicit approval since it is highly likely the prospects have successfully used the services or products of these companies personally. Therefore, they make the logical assumption that the salesperson's product works successfully.

You could also use as an example a company that has a technical environment similar to the customer's. In this case, the company's name or business is de-emphasized while its technical environment is highlighted. Geographic proximity is a very compelling attribute of a reference. If the customer's company is based in New York, a reference to a company that is based in Los Angeles is not nearly as strong as a reference to one that is based in New York.

The ideal reference is the customer's direct competitor. This example provides the highest level of relevance and the most persuasive argument to use the salesperson's product. The perfect hook of all is a company in the same business, in close geographic proximity, and with the same business initiatives.

These slides need to be tightly scripted and diligently memorized. You need to ensure you can describe them in detail and recite them naturally. Finally, the companies mentioned on these slides need to be happy customers since you are offering them as references.

Section III: Explanations

The third section of the presentation is based on Aristotle's logos, the intellectual appeal to customers. Here the goal is to continue to build credibility by methodically explaining background information and facts behind the customer metaphor slides.

For example, let's say you are selling manufacturing shop floor equipment and one of your customer metaphor slides is about how DuPont saved $20 million in the first year of using your product. In this section you would drill down through critical features of your product that streamlined operations. You could explain in detail how the features work technically that enabled the savings to occur and how they compare to other methods of accomplishing the same tasks.

The explanations section is typically the largest of the presentation. As a rule of thumb, use two slides of information for every customer metaphor slide. However, keep in mind that iPods, television, and the Internet have changed people's attention spans and the way they want information to be presented to them. The best presentations deliver information in small chunks. No single slide should take more than two minutes to cover. If it lasts longer than that, you may lose the audience's attention. Therefore, if a slide takes four minutes to explain, split it into two slides to keep the presentation moving.

Section IV: Suggestions

The typical close to a corporate presentation is a one-slide summary of the major topics that were covered. The salesperson basically says, "I hope we passed the audition." A better way to end a presentation is with a very specific action item that is based on the goal you wanted the presentation to accomplish.

For example, if the goal of the presentation was to make the customer's short list, an appropriate close would be to explain the seven reasons why you believe you should be on the short list. If you are further along in the sales cycle and your goal was to close the deal, walking the customer through the implementation process or explaining your pricing methodology is an appropriate close.

These action items should be worded in the form of one of the two types of suggestions: foreground and background. Foreground suggestions are explicit, but they deflect the source of the request from the demander. For example, you could say, "I spoke to my contacts at DuPont yesterday and told them I was presenting to you today. They extended an invitation to come to their operation for a site visit." Another example of a foreground suggestion might be "*Consumer Digest* recommended our product as the best buy for the money and here's why" or "All of the analyst firms strongly encourage that customers benchmark all the products they are considering."

Background suggestions are indirect. Showing your pricing model is a background suggestion to negotiate price. If earlier in your presentation you described how the customers at DuPont made their decision, what products they evaluated, and why they selected your solution, walking the customer through their implementation process is a background suggestion to make the customer think about implementation. Another example of a background suggestion is "One of my customers tried the other company's product and recently switched to ours." While this background suggestion is more subtle in its delivery, it triggers a more profound emotional reaction as the customers will want you to tell them why.

CONCLUSION

Every experienced newspaper reporter knows that a good story has three key elements: tension, drama, and conflict. Customers facing a major purchase decision experience these same emotions. They always feel an underlying tension because they are never 100 percent certain they are picking the right solution. Tension and conflict exist between selection team members over what to do and what solution to pick. These in turn create drama. Drama continues to build as the salespeople make their arguments and provide conflicting information to refute their competitors' claims.

Disparaging remarks and negative criticism occur whenever there is intense competition for a highly sought after prize. In its report on the 2004 presidential election, the Project for Excellence in Journalism, a press watchdog group affiliated with Columbia University Graduate School of Journalism, said that 36 percent of stories about Bush were negative compared to 12 percent about Kerry.[5] The study looked at 16 newspapers of varying size across the country, four nightly newscasts, three network morning news shows, nine cable programs, and nine web sites through the course of 2004. The report concluded that only 20 percent of stories were positive toward Bush compared to 30 percent of stories about Kerry.

In spite of this negative reporting, George Bush still won the election because the pendulum swings back and forth in decision makers' minds from the logical to the emotional. He was able to naturally connect better with voters than Kerry was, and this is an important lesson for salespeople to understand.

Perhaps the greatest single moment to influence customers during the sales cycle is during the corporate sales presentation. The direct approach to the customer presentation is to talk about me, me, me: my company, my products, my products' features and functions. The indirect approach is based on holistic interactionism or you, you, you (i.e., the prospect): translating how other customers in the prospect's situation have been helped. Describing how customers successfully use products is more compelling than detailed discussions about how products work. Ultimately, it takes a good cowcatcher and a great hook to land the really big accounts.

In this chapter, we also reviewed the importance of balanced communication and how similarly Presidents Reagan and Clinton were wired. However, according to one political analyst, "As for Bill

Clinton, whereas Reagan always kept America at center stage, Clinton used America as the stage itself. While the Reagan presidency was all about America, the Clinton presidency was all about Clinton."[6] The lesson for salespeople from this is that it's not about you; it's actually about everyone else but you. You'll win when you help others win.

PART THREE

Common-Sense Tips

PLATO, THE FATHER of Western philosophy, was the originator of the term *common sense*. One of his five branches of philosophy was epistemology, how we gain knowledge about the world around us. Since ancient times, storytelling has been a traditional way of passing knowledge and common sense from generation to generation. In fact, the Greek roots of epistemology are *epistēmē* (knowledge) and *logos* (speech).

All salespeople love to tell stories. We are eager to recount the brilliance of our victories, lament our losses out loud, and share funny tales about our misadventures. The stories we tell provide valuable lessons and tips that can help other salespeople close more business and anticipate trouble. The practical advice these stories provide serves as the foundation for common sense. Like a parent's warning to a child to stay away from a hot stove, guidance from senior salespeople helps the less experienced avoid needless pain and unwanted misery.

The stories and advice in this part cover a broad range of sales-related topics and come from a surprising array of sources—from scientific journals to personal ads. The stories are grouped into lessons about sales and the life of a salesperson. Perhaps the most interesting anecdotes in this part come from the salespeople I have met over the years. So sit back, relax, and pretend you are listening to your colleagues talk about winning and losing and the life of a salesperson.

CHAPTER 6

Common-Sense Selling

> My philosophy of life is that if we make up our mind what
> we are going to make of our lives, then work hard toward
> that goal, we never lose—somehow we win out.
>
> —RONALD REAGAN
> *Reagan, in His Own Hand*

Along with deep discussions about the essence of enlightenment, Buddha offered practical tips to help people with their
daily lives. In the five points of the "purification of the mind," he
argued that people could become free from their suffering.[1] First,
he said your ideas should be based on careful observation and you
should seek to understand cause and effect correctly. Second, your
mistaken observations will be eliminated when information from
your senses is validated by fact. Third, all things have a proper usage, or in today's terms, use the right tool for the job. Fourth, you
need to learn endurance, and finally, you need to be able to spot and
avoid danger. These common-sense tips are just as applicable today
as they were thousands of years ago.

This chapter contains common-sense sales tips and easy-to-
understand advice intended to help you close more business. It is
composed primarily of metaphors—stories, parables, and analogies that communicate ideas by using examples people can relate
to. Similar to the way Buddha, Jesus, and Reagan told stories,
these metaphors are intended to impart important life lessons, introduce complex new ideas, and persuade people to change.

CESSPOOL

A salesperson was presenting his forecast in front of his teammates and was explaining why a deal that he had originally forecasted in the second quarter closed three months later. Here's Brian's story.

Brian was excited that the account he had worked on for months had selected his solution. After several weeks of ensuing price negotiations, a $300,000 purchase order was submitted into the customer's capital expenditure software system (referred to by the customer internally as the "CES system"). Since several weeks were left in the second quarter, Brian expected that he would receive the purchase order well before the quarter's cutoff.

In Brian's mind the deal was done. The purchase order would be printed and signed and he forecasted the deal accordingly. However, Brian was quite surprised to learn that the rules-based CES system required that a purchase of that magnitude be approved by 21 different people. The purchase order had entered the cesspool of order approval.

Between vacations and busy schedules, it would take another three months before all 21 signatures were gathered. In the meantime, Brian embarrassingly had to explain to his manager why a deal he had positively guaranteed would close within the quarter wouldn't.

His assumption about the purchase order turnaround time was dead wrong. If only he'd had the foresight to ask about the details of the procurement process before he committed the deal on his forecast. But as the old saying goes, "If ifs and buts were candy and nuts, oh, what a world this would be."

Tip: Ascertain the customer's procurement process with the same diligence you devote to understanding the customer's selection process.

WHO ARE YOU?

Many salespeople really don't know who attends their sales presentations. Even though introductions are typically made before a meeting starts, full names, exact titles, and complete contact information are rarely collected. Sometimes introductions are made so quickly or the audience is so large that it's impossible to write down all the information. You can't count on attendees to bring business cards. Sometimes the best you can do is remember their first names. Also, people will come in late to the presentation and leave early. It's not practical to stop and ask them who they are and what they do.

One way to keep track of attendees is to create a presentation sign-in sheet. The sheet should have the following columns: name, title, phone number, and e-mail address. A final column should say, "Add to e-mail list? (Y/N)." Pass around the sign-in sheet at the beginning and end of the presentation or whenever someone enters the room. In addition, whether people write *Y* or *N* in the final column is an interesting piece of information about where they stand.

Tip: Keep a couple of presentation sign-in sheets with you at all times so meeting attendees can be correctly identified.

PRICE

Obviously, price is an important purchase factor, and most competent salespeople try to postpone the discussion about price till the end of the sales cycle for good reasons. When you lead with price, you commoditize your product. While it might seem like a good idea to lead with price when yours is the lowest or when your product's capabilities lag behind the competition's, usually this information will be used against you later.

When you lead with price, the customer has leverage since you haven't had a chance to establish the strategic value of your product. Telling exactly how much your solution costs up front can only generate a negative response. In some cases customers will say that it is too expensive and beyond their budget. They'll demand a price concession before they will continue evaluating your solution, long before the final pricing negotiations. Sometimes they'll make a preliminary cut of vendors based solely on this one piece of information.

The 800-pound gorilla in your market space actually sets the yardstick for price, and everyone else is at a disadvantage. If your price is too low, customers will think your product is cheap. If it's too high, customers will think you are a charlatan and it's not worth their time to talk with you. (Customers always believe they can talk the gorilla's price down.)

I have learned a lot about the impact of price from observing how people buy my books. Readers can buy them directly from my web site at the list price, at bookstores often at 30 percent off the list price, or through Internet bookstores at 40 percent off the list price. In reality, the influence of price is circumstantial. If you are at an airport bookstore, for example, you'll gladly pay more for the book than when you have the luxury of time to compare prices on the Internet. In addition, people who buy my book from my web site at full price are 20 times more likely to send me an e-mail with their comments after they have read it. It seems when there is a personal connection, a customer will spend more.

Tip: Always try to postpone the discussion about price, and then have that discussion with someone who has a personal connection with you or your product.

SEVEN REASONS WHY INDY RACE CAR DRIVING IS LIKE SALES

Over the years I have met some pretty interesting people on airplanes—people both famous and unknown, from all walks of life.

One of the most fascinating conversations I ever had was with a fellow named Scott Goodyear. We were seated next to each other on a flight to Indianapolis and started chatting. When I asked him what he did for a living, he replied that he was a former Indy race car driver who now works as a television race commentator. For the next three hours we had the most fascinating discussion about racing and life in general. As he spoke about his racing days, I could not help thinking how much selling and racing in the Indianapolis 500 are alike.

- You must understand the fundamental laws of your field. Indy race car driving is very different from other types of racing. Whereas a NASCAR driver wants to stay close behind another racer in order to draft, the Indy racer needs separation and "clean air" to keep the car from careening out of control. The aerodynamic shape of the car's bottom actually creates suction that keeps the car on the track.

- Peer pressure is huge. The most stressful time for an Indy driver is actually not the race itself. It's the time trials to determine who will take the pole position. During these trials, racers watch their competitors. Specifically, they are looking at what each driver does heading into the first turn and whether he keeps the gas pedal floored. This is the measuring stick that drivers use to determine who's a real contender.

- Racing is a mental sport in which you do what comes naturally. Scott competed in 97 professional races. He quit racing when it didn't feel natural anymore.

- You are part of a fraternity. Indy drivers share a unique camaraderie and a deep respect for one another. While they may be ruthless adversaries on the track, off the track they'll help each other. For example, Scott's advice is highly sought after by current drivers.

- You must constantly improve in everything. I got the impression that Scott was perhaps his own worst critic. He could probably recall every race he was in and what he could have done better.

- You have to take risks to achieve success. Driving more than two hundred miles an hour is risky business. Scott was in several nasty accidents and broke his back on one occasion. However, you can't win races if you don't take chances.

- Winning is everything. Second place doesn't really matter, and Scott should know. He came in second in the closest race in Indianapolis 500 history. Although Scott lost by just a couple of feet and only .43 of a second, Al Unser Jr.'s name is on the winner's trophy.

Similar to race car drivers, salespeople who don't understand the fundamental laws of selling will crash and burn on deals more frequently than they will win them. Selling requires the same mental stamina as professional race car driving, and Heavy Hitters in both professions do what comes naturally. Salespeople belong to a fraternity as well, where colleagues keep watch on how much business you're closing. Heavy Hitters hold themselves to a higher standard, always seeking to improve their performance and never fearing to take calculated risks. After all, winning is everything.

Tip: If sales is your chosen profession, you must treat it like a profession and continually improve your skills. Heavy Hitters know that to stay on top they must never stop learning.

DON'T PANIC

In the battle of Camden, New Jersey, during the Revolutionary War, two-thirds of the Continental Army fled from the king's troops without firing a shot. The story of the battle offers a perspective on the power of fear.

About 3,000 regular troops of the British army had marched through the night to square off against 3,300 American troops. As night turned to day, the frightened Americans could barely make out the British line advancing in their direction. As their enemy moved closer, they saw the more experienced British soldiers form precise battle formations with disciplined precision.

The angst of the Americans quickly built as the British continued their confident, steady march, firing their weapons as they advanced. The Virginian troops threw down their weapons first and fled, followed closely by the North Carolinians and then the entire militia. An American colonel would later write, "He who has never seen the effect of a panic upon a multitude can have but an imperfect idea of such a thing. The best disciplined troops have been enervated and made cowards by it. Armies have been routed by it, even where no enemy appeared to furnish an excuse. Like electricity, it operates instantly; like sympathy, it is irresistible where it touches."[2]

Tip: One of the most important rules in all of sales is not to panic. Regardless of the situation, always keep your head or you won't be able to think your way out. Take General Patton's advice and "Do not take counsel of your fears."[3]

PEER PRESSURE

My 16-year-old daughter just received her driver's license. The state of California has enacted some new laws for first-time drivers like her. For example, for the first year she cannot drive with anyone under the age of 18 in her car, with the exception of immediate family. This new law was put into effect mainly to counteract peer pressure. A study by the National Institute of Child

Health and Development found that teenage boys were twice as likely to crash when they had one other teen with them, and the risk was five times higher with two or more peer passengers. Teenagers were also more likely to drive over the speed limit and tailgate when they had teen passengers, the study concluded.[4]

Peer pressure is just as important an influencer for customers as it is for teenage drivers. It plays a powerful role during the decision-making process. People naturally don't want to look stupid or embarrass themselves in public. Most technical people are very reluctant to admit they don't understand something because doing so could affect their position within the group, particularly in a presentation environment that includes not only their peers but also management.

Selection team members constantly monitor the attitudes of others. Most of the time they will acquiesce to peer pressure in public but may disagree in private. Therefore, when you ask at the end of your presentation, "Does everyone believe we are the best solution?" even though everyone nods, the audience probably includes objectors who will try to sabotage your deal later.

Tip: Peer pressure is part of every sales call. Therefore, you need to closely monitor customers' attitudes and create positive peer pressure to purchase your product.

LESSONS LEARNED

Following every U.S. combat military action, the commanding officer prepares an after-action report that describes in detail what happened during the battle. The final sections of the report highlight what worked well and where improvements are needed, under the subheading "Lessons Learned." In that spirit, here are some of the lessons I have learned about win-loss analysis over the past few years.

- Most salespeople don't take the time to truly understand why they won a deal. They may assume it's because of their product's superior functionality or the effectiveness of their marketing propaganda, but most of the time this isn't the case. They really don't know what was on the customer's mind.

- Most salespeople don't take the time to figure out why they lost a deal. They either don't know why they weren't selected or reflexively blame it on factors out of their control. They really don't know what was on the customer's mind.

- Most sales managers don't correctly relay important win-loss information from the field back to headquarters. Not only do they collect the wrong information, but they usually use it to promote their personal agendas. They really don't know what was on the customer's mind.

True win-loss analysis is very important, and unfortunately, it's a lost art—because no one truly knows what is on the customer's mind.

Tip: The most important information you should know is the truth about why customers do and don't buy your product.

THE FANTASY OF SPAM

Although I have state-of-the-art e-mail filtering software on my computer, I still receive all kinds of spam. These e-mails range from ads for Rolex watches to pitches for Viagra, but each spam message can be classified into one of two categories: needs-based spam and fantasy-based spam. As you read the following e-mails, try to determine whether they are based on a need or a fantasy.

Subject: Apply 70% discounts on software
Top quality software!

Special Offer #1:
Windows: XP Professional+Microsoft Office XP Professional Only $80

Special Offer #2:
Adobe: Photoshop 7, Premiere 7, Illustrator 10 Only $120

Special Offer #3:
Macromedia: Dreamweaver MX 2004+Flash MX 2004 Only $100

Subject: Important message from Barrister Trevor Smithson

Dear Sir,

I am Barrister Trevor Smithson, an accredited attorney with the Head Office of Trust Bank in Nigeria. To be brief, there is a certain amount of money belonging to a client of mine, engineer Morten Smith, your fellow countryman. He died here in Nigeria, leaving no one as an inheritor to his assets.

His personal banker in the bank is a good friend of mine, and he advised me to look for who will be a person capable to stand as his next of kin in order to present him or her to the bank so that his $5,000,000US can be transferred. The sharing will be 50/50. When you confirm your readiness to be a partner to this deal, you will be guided accordingly. Expecting to hear from you as soon as possible.

Yours,
Barrister Trevor Smithson

The first e-mail is needs based, and its success depends on catching customers at the precise moment that they have a specific need to fill. In this case, it is a need for Microsoft, Adobe, or Macromedia software. The second e-mail is fantasy based. It is intended to stir the dreams, hopes, and desires of the reader. Notice how the needs-based spam is focused on price. The spammer is not trying to educate the customer on any of the products. The products are basically commodities. Meanwhile, the fantasy-based spam is intended to drive action by appealing to the imagination. To be successful, it has to educate and influence.

Tip: Do you sell based on price or personal fantasies? Remember, all buyers have secret desires, and they will select the product that brings them the most happiness.

CLIFFS NOTES

As you read the first part of this book, you may have recognized Sun Tzu's most famous quote: "If you know the enemy and know yourself, you need not fear the result of a hundred battles. If you know yourself but not the enemy, for every victory gained you will suffer a defeat. If you know neither the enemy nor yourself, you will succumb in every battle."[5] This is a quote that many salespeople can recite from memory. While it distills Sun Tzu's *Art of War* to its essence, I would like to offer you a modern-day, Cliffs Notes type interpretation of his quote in my own words: "Know your zone."

Basically, every deal is in one of three zones: your zone, a competitor's zone, or open business that is up for grabs. Fifteen percent or so of business is in your zone, meaning it's yours to lose. Most likely, your competitor's zone is similar in size to yours. However, you cannot win there, so you shouldn't even try.

The remaining deals, representing the lion's share of business, should be hotly contested because there is a path for you to win them. All you have to do is figure it out before your competition does.

In your zone is a natural combination of human chemistry, business synergy, and technical fit between you and the customer. This is your sweet spot. Heavy Hitters know their sweet spot inside and out. One might say, for example, "My sweet spot is packaged-goods companies with $250 million to $400 million in annual revenues where the key decision maker is a gregarious 55-year-old male former factory worker who rose through the ranks and is now on a mission to increase plant efficiency." The more specifically you can describe your zone, the better off you are.

Your competitor has a sweet spot as well, and it may be quite close to or far away from your zone. Continuing the example, the competitor's zone might be billion-dollar-revenue packaged-goods companies where the key decision maker is an introverted 45-year-old female who has an extensive financial background.

So, what is your zone? Where are you strong and where are you weak? Equally important, ask these same two questions about your competitor before you decide to work on an account.

Minimize mistakes when working on a deal in your zone. Apply your strengths against the competition's weakness in open accounts. Stay out of deals in the competitor's zone. Salespeople who willingly compete on the enemy's terrain are only fooling themselves. Sales managers who mandate that salespeople go after accounts deep in the competition's zone are just plain foolish.

Tip: The most important question to ask yourself before you start working on a deal is, Is it in your zone or your competitors', or is the business up for grabs?

EXAGGERATORS, SANDBAGGERS, AND HEAVY HITTERS

The old saying that time is money is wrong. Time is actually far more important than money. Time is your most valuable possession. It's also finite. You have only so many days in a month or quarter. That's why I am not a big fan of making salespeople prepare a lot of sales call reports, activity reports, and other forms.

However, I consider one form sacred: the forecast. Your forecast is the measuring stick of your credibility. It is the visible amalgamation of all your years of experience, sales intuition, commitment to your job, and attention to detail. It is also a direct reflection of your character, integrity, and work ethic.

Through the years I have found three basic types of forecasters: exaggerators, sandbaggers, and Heavy Hitters. Exaggerators have what I call "happy ears." They take customers' words at face value. When asked by their manager why they have committed a particular deal to the forecast, they will say, "The customer told us they like our solution." They seem to have forgotten the old adage "All buyers are liars."

Other exaggerators are rose-colored forecasters who interpret every piece of information in their favor. For example, a customer might say, "We understand your product, so there's no reason for you to demonstrate it." The exaggerators will interpret this as a positive sign, even though all the other vendors are demonstrating their products.

Exaggerators continually paint the future as being so incredibly bright that management is hesitant to fire them. While this quarter might not look so good, for exaggerators, the next one is always going to be fantastic. They are so convincing that it takes management several quarters to catch on to the ruse.

Sandbaggers are secretive forecasters who try to give as little information as possible on the forecast. They figure the less information they give, the less exposure they have to management's questions.

Heavy Hitters forecast according to their conscience. Regardless of whether they will have a good or bad quarter, they tell the truth. They ignore the braggadocio and exaggerated forecasts of their teammates and consider it a personal obligation to be honest to themselves, their managers, and the company.

Tip: Preparing a complete, accurate forecast is more than a chore that comes with being in sales; it's proof you belong in sales.

THE SEVEN DEADLY SINS OF SALESPEOPLE

In the late sixth century, Pope Gregory described the seven deadly sins, from the least serious to the most, as *superbia, invidia, ira, avaritia, tristia, gula,* and *luxuria.* Translated from Latin, they are pride, envy, anger, avarice, sadness, gluttony, and lust. What do you think are the seven deadly sins of salespeople? Here's my list, in order of least to most severe.

- *Chattering.* Salespeople talk too much on sales calls for a variety of reasons. Some are nervous chatterers who just can't keep their mouths shut. Others think they know more than the customer so they lecture the customer to death. Many salespeople feel compelled to recite their canned pitch regardless of the customer's actual interest. You have conducted a perfect sales call when the customer has been persuaded to buy even though you listened far more than you spoke.

- *Gourmandizing.* Millionaire railroad tycoon Diamond Jim Brady was a legendary gourmand who lived at the turn of the twentieth century. For breakfast he ate eggs, pancakes, pork chops, cornbread, fried potatoes, hominy, muffins, and beefsteak, and drank a gallon of orange juice. Lunch consisted of two lobsters, deviled crabs, clams, oysters, beef, and several pies. A platter of seafood and carafes of lemon soda constituted his 4:30 snack. The evening meal began with three dozen oysters, six crabs, and turtle soup. The main course was two whole ducks, six or seven lobsters, a sirloin steak, and servings of vegetables. Dessert included a platter of pastries and often a two-pound box of candy.[6] Does your sales organization include a "Diamond Jim Brady" who devours company resources to the point of gluttony?

- *Inactivity.* Salespeople must be short-term thinkers and long-term planners. An inactive salesperson neglects the future and does not spend time on activities that build his future pipeline. Inactivity is not to be confused with laziness. Many hardworking salespeople are completely focused on the here and now. Unfortunately, they forget about next quarter and next year. Other salespeople place all their eggs in one basket, never really thinking about what will happen if their big deal collapses. They have been lulled into a state of inactivity and could be jolted into reality at any moment.

- *Obliviousness.* Many salespeople don't take the time to understand how customers fit within their own organization. I am continually amazed at the lackadaisical attitude many salespeople have about understanding the organizational structure of the companies they call on. When they are asked what a person's title is, they will answer, "manager," or something equally nebulous, when they should answer, "manager of application security who reports to the director of application development, who, in turn, reports to the CIO."

- *Shallowness.* Salespeople who don't know their product well enough to build customer credibility cannot be expected to drive account strategy. How can you determine your next course of action if you don't understand the customer's technical objections and how best to emphasize the product's strengths? Worse, in this situation you are completely at the mercy of someone else because another member of your company has to explain how your product works.

- *Presumptuousness.* Assuming information you really don't know is one of the worst sins for a salesperson. Salespeople who are not certain but make their best guess about who the bully with the juice is are more than halfway to losing the deal.

- *Ignorance.* Ignorance is the deadliest sin. If you do not have a "spy" within an account who is telling you what is happening in closed-door meetings, defending you when you are not around, and disseminating propaganda on your behalf, you will most certainly lose.

Tip: Your success is your responsibility. The road to the top is paved with hard work, diligence, and self-discipline.

GO, FIGHT, WIN!

While I am not a sports fanatic, I have followed one team since I was a boy. I've always had a special affinity for the University of Southern California Trojans football team (on which my dad played). Therefore, it's no surprise that one of my favorite football coaches of all time is John McKay. McKay reached the highest heights by winning five national championships at USC and the lowest lows with the longest losing streak in National Football League history while at Tampa Bay. Through it all, he never lost his sense of humor.

When the pressure is always on to win, having a sense of humor is not only important but mandatory as a way to release tension. Off the field, McKay was one of the wittiest coaches ever. For example, following a loss, when a reporter asked what he thought of the team's execution, he said, "I think it's a good idea." After another loss, he said, "We didn't tackle, but we made up for it by not blocking."[7]

McKay recalled the situation after Notre Dame's 51–0 victory over USC in 1966: "The toughest part about this coaching business is always having something to say to your team after a loss. So, I said, 'All of you who need showers, take them. The rest of you, get dressed. And remember this, a billion Chinese won't even know we played Notre Dame.' The next day I got two telegrams from Peking and they both said, 'What happened?' "[8]

The best football game I ever attended was USC versus Notre Dame in 1974. With Notre Dame leading 24–6 at halftime, the Irish fans in the stands were already celebrating their victory and taunting the hometown USC crowd. McKay told his team in the locker room at halftime, "If you knock down 11 players, A.D. [Anthony Davis] will run it back all the way. Hell, if you knock down all 11 Notre Dame guys, I could run it back, you could run it back."[9] When the second half started, A.D. ran back the opening kickoff and USC scored 55 unanswered points in 17 minutes to win. Coming from behind to win is a mark of true character.

Today, USC has another great coach. Pete Carroll has accomplished a stunning turnaround of the program. He won back-to-back national championships in 2004 and 2005, and his team set a new record for the number of weeks it was ranked number one in the country.

When you analyze why USC is winning, it comes down to three main reasons. First, the players are having fun. Having fun begets winning, and winning begets having fun. One player commented, "Coach Carroll makes it intense and fun. I don't think enough coaches realize how bad it looks to the players when they stand on the sideline like somebody just died. Coach Carroll gives us enthusiasm that we can feed off."[10]

Second, Pete Carroll has minimized the factors out of his control and maximized those within his control. Recruiting new players is completely within his control; therefore, recruiting is his number one focus. He hires the best assistant coaches and recruits the most talented players. No program can sustain success without continually upgrading its talent. Since the most talented team members play, including freshmen, the survival-of-the-fittest environment keeps all the players on their toes.

Finally, the coach and players have an insatiable appetite for winning. They aren't resting on their laurels. In the words of Pete Carroll, "There is no end. There is no eureka. You just keep going."[11]

Sports and sales share a lot of the same characteristics. Each requires hard work, perseverance, sacrifice, and personal discipline. More importantly, each is based on preparing oneself—physically, mentally, and strategically—for the long run, whether it is an entire season or a fiscal year.

Pete Carroll's story has another lesson for salespeople. Before he took over the USC program, he was a head coach in the National Football League (NFL). His record leading the New York Jets for a season was 6–6, and for the two seasons he spent with the New England Patriots his record was 27–21. The same man who was regarded as a mediocre coach is now one of the most admired in the nation. This provides a very important point. Your success is dependent upon your ability to find an environment where you can be successful, one that fits your personal strengths and your own particular style.

Tip: Unfortunately, too many sales environments are based only on intensity with little or no fun. Add some fun and humor to your routine and you'll find you lose less often. You'll also enjoy your job more if you focus on the factors you can control and don't lament the ones you can't.

FIVE QUESTIONS TO ASK AFTER A LOSS

When we're closing business, life's great! But when we're on the losing side of a deal, we can feel like our entire world has fallen apart. Losing is a subject that most salespeople don't like to talk about. However, unless we truly understand why we lose, we will most assuredly lose again.

While losing to competitors is painful, losing to the dreaded "no decision" is even worse: we spent time, effort, and resources on an account where the selection team couldn't even make a decision. Whether losing to competitors or to no decision, true loss analysis starts by asking five fundamental questions that are inherent to every sale.

Question 1: Did We Sell to the Bully with the Juice?

Some people are natural-born leaders. They command respect, and people tend to follow their lead. Such a person is the bully with the juice. In every deal, only one person is the bully with the juice and the sole decision maker.

It is imperative to identify with absolute certainty who is the bully with the juice. Obviously, a top priority is to meet this decision maker in order to understand his or her needs, ascertain biases, and persuade the person to choose your solution. If you can't determine who is the bully with the juice, you should be prepared to lose. Likewise, always assume the bully with the juice is meeting with your competitors as well.

Question 2: Did We Sell Logically or Psychologically?

Unfortunately, we have been trained to think of customers and ourselves as rational decision makers who use logic and reason exclusively. However, every major purchase decision can be traced to one of four psychological roots: the will to survive, the desire to avoid pain, the need to gain approval of others, and the desire to satisfy selfish egos.

When you sell based solely upon logic, you are destined to lose because the logical reasons people give for buying products are only rationalizations that enable them to justify the expenditure. The successful influencer is the one who appeals to the four psychological motivators.

Question 3: Did We Know the Decision Maker's Fantasy?

All sales involve selling the fantasy that a product is going to make the customer's life easier, save the customer money, or enable the customer to make more money. The feature set of your product validates the fantasy elements of your story and promotes the customer's fantasy. During the sales cycle, your goal is to communicate how you can turn your customer's fantasy into a reality, but only when your product is selected.

Selection team members also have personal fantasies. Maybe they want to master new technology to enrich their resumes. Maybe they want to earn bonuses for cutting costs or increasing revenue. Maybe they want to be perceived as heroes within the company or to spend more time at home and less at work. Everyone has a personal fantasy that is associated with the procurement of a product. Heavy Hitters understand this and align their strategy with personal fantasies. They don't just recite product features, benefits, and specifications.

Question 4: Did We Have a Spy in the Account?

All successful sales involve a salesperson being coached through the evaluation process by an internal "spy." You need a spy within the account to win the deal. This person is a constant source of accurate information revealing the internal machinations of the customer's selection process.

The ideal spy is the person with the highest authority or greatest influence who is involved in the selection process. When this person becomes a spy, the salesperson will enjoy a unique advantage. However, the spy could be anybody inside the customer's company or even someone outside the company, such as a consultant involved in the selection process and the implementation of the winning vendor's product.

Why would someone help one salesperson versus another? Because one salesperson was able to establish a personal relationship. To establish a personal relationship with a spy, Heavy Hitters build different types of rapport with the customer. At the foundation is a special relationship based on personal rapport between two individuals who like each other. Although powerful, this personal rapport is meaningless unless technical rapport is present. Technical rapport is achieved when a product's features satisfy the customer's features and functions requirements. Finally, before the deal can be consummated, business rapport must be achieved such that the customer believes the salesperson's company has the expertise to solve the customer's problems.

Heavy Hitters manage their time by qualifying people. They know that before they work on an account, they need to determine if they can find someone within the customer's company who will help them win the deal. If they can't develop such a contact, they know it does not make sense to invest their time in the account.

Question 5: Did We Build Personal Relationships with the Customer?

Regardless of how many people surround someone or how much fortune, fame, and power you think a person has, everyone is lonely in his or her own way. Loneliness isn't only about being alone. It is feeling disconnected, isolated, alienated, unwanted, inadequate, self-conscious, and unloved. Every decision maker is uniquely lonely, and the deal winner is the salesperson who is best able to build a mutual friendship.

I admire persistent salespeople and respect the underdog who will fight with passion and battle against the odds. However, sometimes it's impossible to win. Such is the case when your competitor has such a tight grip on an account that there is no way to break it. In some accounts, although you may not be told so directly, the customer simply doesn't like you.

Even facing these circumstances, some salespeople believe the customer is just playing hard to get or treating every vendor the same way (which isn't true). These salespeople mistakenly believe they can turn the situation around by sheer willpower and determination. Recognizing when to abandon an account is as important as knowing what accounts to pursue. Ultimately, you will win deals only where you are given the opportunity to build personal relationships.

Tip: Customers are smarter at buying products and more skeptical than ever. In addition, product differentiation is at an all-time low. Ultimately, you must sell customers something much larger—the idea that you can help change their lives for the better, enable them to be a part of something greater than themselves, and partner with them for the long term.

ARE YOU CONTAGIOUS?

If you were to ask a hundred different salespeople who sell complex solutions to describe their selling approach, one of the most frequent responses would be "consultative." Simply put, this sales approach is based on establishing oneself as a business expert who sets out to understand and solve the customer's business problems. Like a consultant, the salesperson studies the customer's environment and applies industry knowledge to create a solution that theoretically differentiates the salesperson from the competition.

Obviously, it is better to have the customer think of you as a business expert than to think you're a money-grubbing salesperson, so this approach makes sense. And when it was introduced over a decade ago, it was unique. Unfortunately, most of your competitors are employing this approach today. Worse, most salespeople confuse the consultative approach with an actual sales strategy, which it isn't. It is only a communication tactic to establish your credibility and deliver your information in a nonthreatening way.

Most salespeople know how to sell logically only. This is not surprising because we have been trained throughout our careers to think of customers as rational, logical decision makers. Our companies tell us to qualify the customer's business requirements, such as budget and time frame to buy, and find out the product features and functions that the customer needs. They arm us with facts and specifications so that we can launch informational assaults on customers in order to get them to buy. Since most companies understand only this type of direct approach, they train salespeople in direct battlefield maneuvers and the recitation of features, functions, and specifications. No training covers the essence of the indirect strategy—how to win hearts and minds of the customers.

I once interviewed members of a customer team who said the main reason they made a million-dollar purchase was that the salesperson was "contagious." That's a very interesting term, so I asked them to define it. They told me that they had looked at a half-dozen different solutions, and all of the salespeople they met with were equally professional and courteous. They even commented that each played the role of salesperson very well. The salespeople displayed interest in understanding the customer's needs and requirements, were able to explain how their products would meet those require-ments, and were responsive during the selection process. While some products were slightly better than others, all were relatively the same from a feature and price standpoint.

Some salespeople were better liked than others, but no one re-ally stood out except Bob. He was different. He wasn't just repre-senting his company; the team members felt that he *was* the company. In essence, they felt that he honestly believed in what he was doing and saying. When I asked them if he had the best product, was charismatic or good-looking, or had some other unique advantage, the answer they gave was surprising. They said he was a nondescript fellow and his product ranked low on the list of capabilities.

Instead, the reason why Bob won was that he was completely comfortable with himself. In essence, he was transparent. The cus-tomers really knew who he was. For them, making a million-dollar purchase was a nerve-racking experience. Bob's genuine enthusi-asm, appreciation of people, and love of his company became a magnet. While the customers had laid out a laundry list of specifi-cations each vendor's product had to meet, the emotional reasons for the decision far outweighed the logical reasons in the end. They were looking for peace of mind during the selection process. Equally important, they wanted someone around they believed in.

Tip: The most persuasive salesperson is completely sold on his company, product, and most importantly, himself.

ALWAYS FOLLOW YOUR INTUITION

The following passage is from the National Commission on Terror-ist Attacks' 2004 report: "A special note on the importance of trust-ing subjective judgment: One potential hijacker was turned back by an immigration inspector as he tried to enter the United States.

The inspector relied on intuitive experience to ask questions more than he relied on any objective factor that could be detected by 'scores' or a machine. Good people who have worked in jobs for a long time understand this phenomenon well."[12]

Some people equate their intuition with gut feelings. However, your intuition is far more complex than that. It actually is a powerful decision-making model that takes into account all your past experiences, the information you have consciously gathered about the particular situation you're facing, and your subconscious mind's silent advice. Sometimes your intuition provides instant feedback and makes the hair on the back of your neck stand up. Usually it's more subtle and takes some time to manifest itself.

Ronald Reagan used to take long showers to tap into his psyche. Jesus Christ would slip away from the throngs of followers to be alone with his thoughts. Meditation and thought control are at the heart of Buddha's teachings. In the same way, every salesperson needs "think time."—a daily time to be completely alone, deliberate on different possible scenarios, and ponder what's important. Whether you're at work, traveling, or at home, quality think time will help you to tap into your intuition. And remember, always follow your intuition.

Tip: You can't hear your intuition if you don't make the time to listen for it. Set aside some daily time to think about important deals and contemplate your next action.

BOY, WERE THEY WRONG!

In 1899, the commissioner of the U.S. Office of Patents stated publicly that everything that could be invented had been invented. In 1922, the U.S. postmaster general called airplanes an impractical fad with no serious place in postal transportation. A movie executive advised against investing in the motion picture *Gone with the Wind* because no Civil War picture had ever made a dime. In 1982, IBM did not buy Microsoft for $100 million because it was too expensive.[13]

Albert Einstein's teacher wrote to his father that he would never amount to anything. A concert manager told Elvis Presley after one of his first concerts to go back to driving a truck. A Yale University professor gave the paper that proposed the concept of creating Federal Express a grade of C because the idea was not feasible.[14]

Tip: If you are going to make a mistake, make sure it's a little one, not a big one, and never, ever count people out.

WARNING SIGNS

I recently read an article that listed the 13 warning signs that you may be suffering from job burnout. How many of these symptoms do you experience?

1. Chronic fatigue: exhaustion, tiredness, a sense of being physically run down.

2. Anger at those making demands of you.

3. Self-criticism for putting up with the demands.

4. Cynicism, negativity, and irritability.

5. A sense of being besieged.

6. Exploding easily at seemingly inconsequential things.

7. Frequent headaches and gastrointestinal disturbances.

8. Weight loss or gain.

9. Sleeplessness and depression.

10. Shortness of breath.

11. Suspiciousness.

12. Feelings of helplessness.

13. Increased degree of risk taking.[15]

The premise of the article was that if you frequently have any of these symptoms, then you are most likely in the wrong job. It recommended making a change because you are working at something you weren't designed to do. It provided the analogy that you wouldn't use a fork to dig a trench.

However, this premise as it applies to salespeople is fundamentally wrong. Most salespeople experience symptoms like these on a regular basis. In fact, they are inherent to sales and should be accepted as such. Usually, they come and go in cycles, typically in relation to the amount of business that is being closed.

When we experience fear, depression, and self-doubt, we tend to avoid people and separate ourselves from those whom we are close to, believing that we have to pick ourselves up through our own willpower. But the best way to defeat the doldrums is exactly the opposite. Instead of withdrawing into yourself, you should actually commiserate with your colleagues and seek their support.

All salespeople know despondency and despair intimately. Sharing your angst and frustrations with fellow salespeople will help you get back on your feet sooner. Instead of continuing self-defeating thoughts, engaging in catharsis enables you to let go of your negativity. Your spirits will rise as soon as you realize that you are not alone in your circumstances. Your sales will bounce back sooner, too.

Tip: Think about the greatest moments of your life. Did they happen while you were alone? Most likely they didn't. You were probably surrounded by people during all of the greatest moments of your life. And surrounding yourself with people during tough times is even more important than on the momentous occasions.

TEST YOUR SELLING STYLE

Your selling style is influenced by a complex combination of your instinctive drives. You naturally use these instincts to exert your will upon customers. Nine basic instincts determine your selling style and your actions at any particular moment. The nine instincts are dominance, hyperactivity, pride, greed, freedom, transparency, curiosity, empathy, and modeling.

We can group these sales instincts into three categories: survival (dominance, hyperactivity, pride, and greed); creativity (freedom, transparency, and curiosity); and intuition (empathy and modeling). Whereas the survival instincts are associated with attack and defense, the creative instincts have more to do with achievement and self-worth. Meanwhile, your intuition enables you to read minds and predict the future. Let's review each of these instincts in more detail.

Survival Instincts: Dominance, Hyperactivity, Pride, and Greed

The drive to take command of a situation (dominance) is instrumental in a salesperson's success. Some salespeople have such a strong dominance instinct that they think of customers as naturally inferior people. Conversely, a salesperson with a weak dominance instinct is more apt to operate under the direction of customers. However, you should seek the equilibrium point between dominance and submission for each account. It's the point where the customer respects your conviction and is not offended by your persistence.

You can think of the instinct of hyperactivity as your sales metabolism, the pace at which you work your territory. Some salespeople can't stop moving. They're always talking on the phone, sending e-mail messages, or making contacts. They're nervous and uncomfortable when events aren't humming along actively. Other salespeople are more deliberate in their moves, and they take longer to complete the same sorts of activities. Whether one pace is better than the other depends on the nature of the deals you must compete for.

You may not have initially thought of pride as an instinct, but it is one. Pride is the measure of self-importance and your opinion of your own worth. Pride is also the midway point between arrogance and humility. Since arrogant salespeople think they already know all the answers, they are less likely to ask for direction or seek input (from customers and managers alike). In general, arrogance is a very bad attribute for a salesperson. However, some products actually require arrogant salespeople. These products are usually targeted at an elitist clientele.

We normally associate greed with a miserly scrooge or a corrupt character. Whereas this may be society's definition, in sales greed takes on an entirely different meaning. You have probably worked with many different types of salespeople, and you may have noticed that some gravitate toward working on only big deals, while others nickel-and-dime their way to their quotas. The greed instinct is actually a key influencer in the way salespeople work their territories.

Some salespeople aren't afraid of bold decisions and the consequences they entail. They are dreamers who envision the day when their ship will finally come in. They are unfulfilled working on numerous smaller deals. They want to set their line in the deepest water and catch the biggest fish. Meanwhile, other salespeople are quite happy casting their nets closer to shore and snagging as many deals as possible. They are more likely to yield to the opinions of others and play it safe.

Creative Instincts: Freedom, Transparency, and Curiosity

The freedom instinct is actually the measurable state of independence versus dependency and conformity. Assertiveness varies from individual to individual. Some salespeople are opinionated trailblazers, while others are more likely to go along with the crowd. The trailblazers tend to be rebellious salespeople who will fight any battle, regardless of its impact on them. To maintain their independence, they'll vehemently oppose any new sales-related process or procedure. Passive salespeople distance themselves from any confrontation. They quietly set about fulfilling their duties.

Transparency is the ability to be exactly who you are and the propensity to be perfectly frank about it. In other words, what people see is what you are. Some salespeople are completely transparent. They are very comfortable with themselves, let others see exactly who they are, and tell it like it is. Other salespeople tend to display less personality and shield themselves behind a more formal demeanor.

Like people in general, salespeople have different levels of inquisitiveness. Some salespeople have a healthy curiosity and a strong need to know every detail, probably because they have to satisfy their insatiable desire to know the truth: Will I win the deal? Others are more likely to take a customer's words at face value. They won't question the customer outright but will make their own subjective judgment about the truthfulness of the information.

Intuition Instincts: Empathy and Modeling

Male salespeople are more likely to think of empathy as a feminine trait that is much like commiseration. However, empathy is the ability to feel other people's emotions and see from their perspective. Empathy is neither female nor male; its source is actually a cluster of cells called "mirror neurons" in the brains of men and women alike.

When we watch someone else perform an action, mirror neurons fire off and respond as if we were doing it ourselves. Mirror neurons help explain why laughter is contagious, why we grimace in pain for people we don't even know, and why we feel like crying when we see others cry. However, not everyone has the same amount or strength of mirror neurons. As a result, salespeople have different levels of empathy and differing abilities to place themselves in the "mental shoes" of their customers.

Your mind's ability to store information is very sophisticated. Modeling is the ability to link like experiences and similar data into predictable patterns. Salespeople continually learn through the ongoing accumulation and consolidation of information from sales calls and interactions with customers. From this knowledge base, salespeople can predict what will happen and what they should do in light of what they have done in the past.

For example, let's say you were asked by a skeptical, detail-oriented customer how your product is different from your major competitor's. Your answer would be based on your previous experience with similar circumstances. Modeling can be thought of as trying to find the *what, when, where* response — *what you should do when* you are in a particular circumstance *where* you have to act. The ability to combine attributes from different sales calls into themes and models of behavior forms your intuition. The strength of your intuition determines your ability to predict the future.

Now that we have defined each of the nine instincts, take the following test. On a scale of 1 to 5, low to high, circle the number that best represents the strength of each of your instincts. Be honest with yourself. There are no right or wrong answers. Your individual style is based on your personal mixture of these instincts, and you can be successful with any combination.

Survival
    Dominance   1 2 3 4 5
    Hyperactivity   1 2 3 4 5
    Pride   1 2 3 4 5
    Greed   1 2 3 4 5

Creativity
    Freedom   1 2 3 4 5
    Transparency   1 2 3 4 5
    Curiosity   1 2 3 4 5

Intuition
    Empathy   1 2 3 4 5
    Modeling   1 2 3 4 5

Most salespeople find that their answers cluster together in each category. For example, a salesperson with moderate empathy will usually have a moderate modeling instinct. Also, rankings tend to gravitate toward one end of the spectrum in the survival and creative instinct categories. For example, a highly dominant salesperson will most likely have high rankings in pride and greed as well. Conversely, salespeople low in transparency usually score themselves low in freedom and tend to prefer more structured sales environments.

An instinct's higher ranking is not necessarily better or more desirable. That depends on the products you sell and the customers you must interact with. For example, a stockbroker needs to be a hyperactive juggler of multiple transactions, whereas a financial planner for retirees needs to hold meetings at a measured pace. Also, the different instincts work together and complement each other. For instance, a high degree of empathy compensates for a lack of other critical instincts.

Although you can achieve success with any combination of the nine instincts, the most successful salespeople are the ones who are able to span the most diverse range of instincts. They are chameleons who know they must dominate one customer and be submissive to another. Sometimes they follow orders, and other times they question authority. They are comfortable being exactly who they are but can take on any role required to win business.

Tip: To help broaden and improve your instincts, try to spend an entire day acting in a manner that's opposite to the way your instincts are naturally wired. If you are hyperactive, slow down. If you are not very curious, question everything. If you gravitate toward big deals, try working on smaller accounts. You may learn important secrets about yourself and your customer relationships that you weren't even aware of.

CONCLUSION

This chapter includes many metaphors. Metaphors are more than simple anecdotes or interesting fairy tales. Their purpose is to tell, teach, and enlighten listeners or readers with the ultimate goal of changing their behavior. Metaphors facilitate the learning process by enabling people to understand new concepts in terms they already know, and they quickly communicate complex ideas.

More importantly, metaphors are language structures with multiple layers of personal interpretation. They connect logical and psychological meaning together. While on the surface they provide a logical story that the conscious mind follows, their deeper layers can evoke memories, provide insights on how to handle life's problems, and impart suggestions that percolate in the subconscious mind.

Metaphors are one of the most powerful persuasion tools at your disposal. The stories you tell decision makers about customers who are using your product, your company's future plans, and why you chose to work at the company are powerful metaphors. Even the way you dress, present yourself, and represent your product provides important symbolism to the customer. In reality, you are a walking metaphor.

CHAPTER 7

The Life of a Salesperson

My motto has always been, a career open to all talents, without distinctions of birth.

—NAPOLEON BONAPARTE

Napoleon Bonaparte believed in equality. He thought each man should have the opportunity to succeed based solely upon his ability, as he felt he had done. Those who personified this ideal were awarded a special mark of esteem, the five-armed insignia called the Legion of Honor.

The Legion of Honor was intended to reward civilians and soldiers alike. Napoleon said of the award, "Civilian virtues must have their reward as well as military virtues. Force itself is nothing without intelligence. Let us honour intelligence, accomplishments, civilian qualities, in other words, in all professions and let us reward them equally. Soldiers unable to read or write will be proud to wear the same decoration as illustrious scientists. Scholars will attach more value to it because it will be the same for all outstanding men."[1]

Sales is a legion-of-honor profession in which anyone can achieve success. The most unlikely individuals have succeeded when everyone around them thought they would fail. But here's the most important point: Each of us becomes a Heavy Hitter using our own particular style in our own individual way. Those who internalize this fundamental law enjoy long and prosperous careers in sales.

However, the life of a salesperson is far from perfect. Everyone in the profession has trials and tribulations. Salespeople experience incredible highs, tremendous lows, and a constant fear of the unknown. In this chapter, we review the underpinnings necessary for a successful sales career and important lessons about the life of a salesperson.

LONG LUNCH

I once sat through an entire lunch listening to the CEO and founder of a $400 million company debate the nature of sales with his vice president of sales. The technical-minded CEO argued that sales was a process, and in this regard, the sales department should not be run much differently from other departments, like manufacturing. He believed sales just worked with different raw materials and produced a much less predictable output. He argued that when the right processes were established, the end result would be better and more predictable.

The vice president of sales responded that the primary responsibility of his salespeople was to build relationships. He argued that to some extent, it really didn't matter what product they sold. What was important was how well they built relationships because people buy from people.

I kept out of the debate as long as possible. After both sides had exhausted their arguments, they asked me for my opinion on who was right. Without hesitation, I responded that sales is the process of building relationships. If you take a process-oriented view of sales, you will focus only on the process and leave out the most important piece of the puzzle: people. If you believe it is solely about relationships, though, you will never have a blueprint of success others within the sales department can follow. Sales requires an understanding of the basic laws of human nature plus the process of understanding how information is exchanged. Both sides seemed satisfied with the truthfulness of my answer.

Tip: I have never seen a company sign a contract, a check, or a purchase order. It's the people who work for companies who provide their signatures. Sales is the process of building relationships with people.

THE 19.5 REASONS YOU WILL FAIL

A vice president of sales sent an e-mail to his entire sales team titled "The 19.5 reasons why you fail." His list gave his top reasons why his salespeople were failing. Although his intention was to stimulate his team members' thinking and improve their performance, the e-mail had the opposite effect. Every sentence started with either "You fail," "You don't," or "You can't." The e-mail's negative and condescending nature infuriated everyone. Soon the e-mail was posted in chat rooms and on bulletin boards where the vice president was vilified as one of the worst sales leaders of all time.

Here are my thoughts after reading his list. First, it was a terrible misuse of e-mail. Whenever possible, serious announcements should always be done in person, not over the Internet. I am sure the vice president was not too happy when he found out he was being lampooned by thousands of Internet users in spite of his best intentions. Second, he broke the golden rule of sales management, which is to praise in public and critique in private.

Finally, the message was a horrendous use of two of the most important sales resources: time and language. The vice president had obviously put much thought into creating the e-mail and was probably quite pleased with himself when he clicked the Send button. Unfortunately, he had no idea that he was sending a message that actually encouraged failure. Beyond the content of his words, he was brainwashing his team members with the idea that they were failures. Instead of motivating them to succeed for the good and glory of all, the anger his e-mail generated toward a disrespectful boss most likely fueled turmoil and dissension.

Tip: Never send an e-mail or letter that you wouldn't mind seeing printed on the front page of your hometown newspaper.

KEEP PERSPECTIVE

I honestly cannot remember whether the third quarter of 2000 was a good one or a bad one. (I can barely remember what happened just a few quarters ago.) However, I do remember that at the time it was the most important quarter ever and my drive to succeed dominated my thoughts.

What goes up must come down. You will have good and bad quarters, boom and bust years. Similarly, careers experience periods of success and failure. Good times don't last forever, and bad times are never over for sure. In the words of Buddha, "Though he should conquer a thousand men in the battlefield a thousand times, yet he who would conquer himself is the noblest victor."[2]

Tip: To enjoy a long career in sales, you must think of your career over the long term.

ASK THE EXPERTS

If you are in sales, you have no doubt flown on your share of airplanes. Therefore, you should easily know the answer to the following question about the jets you fly so frequently and have seen so often. How many turbine engines do Boeing 727, 737, and 757 planes have? Is the answer two, three, or four?

The answer will probably surprise you, but it is three. You are probably wondering how can that be (especially if you happen to be on one of these planes at the moment and can see only one engine on each of the wings). There's actually a small turbine engine in the tail of the plane. However, this engine is used mainly when the plane is at the terminal to power all of the onboard systems.

How I learned this interesting bit of trivia is the real point of the story. I was flying from Los Angeles to Dallas and happened to be sitting next to a pilot who was deadheading home. I had a lot of work to do, but the opportunity to ask a pilot all of the questions I had about planes and flying was too important to pass up. This was a chance to learn from an expert.

I put all my work on the back burner and interrogated him about every aspect of flying—for example, how wind speed is calculated, what happens when lightning hits the plane, and how the air lane system (highways in the sky) works.

Tip: Being part of a sales force, you are surrounded by more experienced sales experts day in, day out. Take the time to ask them questions and learn from them.

WHY DOES MY SALES MANAGER DISLIKE ME?

Your sales manager can make your life enjoyable, tolerable, or miserable. The following piece, which was the most frequently read article on the Heavy Hitter Selling web site (www.heavyhitter selling.com), illustrates this point.

> Have you ever worked for a sales manager who made you feel uncomfortable? Even though you consistently made your number, it seemed you never earned his or her respect. Although you made many attempts to improve your relationship, they were all met with indifference. Your sales

manager can make your life enjoyable, tolerable, or miser-able, and your mental condition is profoundly influenced by this critical relationship. Understanding your sales man-ager's management style is the key to winning over this cru-cial person.

Over the past 20 years, I have been exposed to hundreds of dif-ferent sales managers while serving as a salesperson, vice president, consultant, and sales trainer. Frankly, I have found many to be very good and a few that were just plain horrible. But I can honestly say I learned as much from the bad ones as from the good ones. More importantly, I began to recognize patterns of behavior and catalog management style tendencies.

Just as people have different levels of gregariousness, assertive-ness, and action-oriented tendencies, they have different sales man-agement styles. I have found that seven management styles are most prevalent. Most likely, a manager has one dominant style. However, he or she will probably share a few characteristics with other styles and may even move from style to style depending on the situation. The seven most common sales management styles are the mentor, expressive manager, sergeant, Teflon manager, amateur manager, micromanager, and overconfident manager.

People with each of these management styles build different sales environments by hiring their type of salespeople and establish-ing a culture based on their belief system and personality. Figure 7.1 lists the seven different sales management styles and the charac-teristics of the sales force environment they create.

Obviously, the cultures a mentor and a micromanager create are quite different. If you worked for a mentor and suddenly found yourself working for a micromanager, you would have to adapt to a completely different style. Conversely, a mentor doesn't have the same priorities or thought processes as a micromanager. You would lose credibility with a mentor if you treated him as though he were a micromanager. Heavy Hitters implement a strategy to build a

Management Style	Sales Force Composition	Cultural Characteristics
Mentor	Scholarly students	Investigative, consultative
Expressive manager	Empathetic egomaniacs	Me first, bravado
Sergeant	Sincere soldiers	Loyal, obedient
Teflon manager	Patient Pollyannas	Optimistic, nice guys and gals
Amateur manager	Schizophrenic salespeople	Unpredictable, unlikable
Micromanager	Perfect performers	Repetitive task orientation
Overconfident manager	Clever conquerors	Win at any cost

Figure 7 1   The Seven Sales Management Styles

long-term relationship based on their sales manager's style. Let's examine each of the sales management styles further and the strategies a Heavy Hitter uses to manage the relationship.

Mentors

Mentors are charismatic leaders and sales experts who measure their success using three criteria: exceeding revenue goals, creating an environment where the entire team can succeed, and helping all team members realize their individual potentials. Mentors are confident in their own abilities and possess the business insight to know what needs to be done and how to do it.

Even though they believe in accountability and a strict code of ethical conduct, they relate well with their team and motivate by positive encouragement rather than fear. They are comfortable with themselves and are able to keep a perspective and a sense of resolution during tenuous times.

The mentors' philosophy is an extension of their personality. While their demeanor may range from gruff and cantankerous to friendly and personable, they are well liked and act as a unifying force to their sales team members. Although mentors tend to have a very hands-on management style, they don't meddle in their teams' daily duties. They lead by example instead.

Salespeople want to learn everything they can from mentors, so they adopt a strategy based on being a scholarly student. They invite their mentors on calls, quiz them about tactics over lunch, or chat with them after hours about their sales experiences. They also extend this strategy to their customers. They want to understand what makes customers tick and the problems they are trying to solve and to befriend them. This becomes the culture of the organization.

Expressive Managers

Expressive managers are people oriented with a flair for sharing their emotions and amplifying the emotions of those around them. They have a natural ability to put people at ease. They are very charming and gregarious individuals who are always ready, willing, and able to discuss personal matters in addition to events at work. They will frequently be seen chatting with coworkers in other departments at the watercooler.

Expressive managers create an environment where a considerable amount of energy is focused on how they are thought of and perceived within the company. They crave attention and tend to be overdramatic, either exaggerating their accomplishments or overstating the prevailing circumstances their team is facing. These so-called sympathy complaints are subconscious attempts to secure love and affection. Expressive managers are saying, "Pay attention to me!" Because of their need for constant emotional approval, they may become jealous when others receive recognition.

The long-term strategy Heavy Hitters employ to shape their relationships with expressive managers is called "empathetic ego." Empathizing with expressive managers requires sharing their experiences through unselfish listening and continual confirmation that the Heavy Hitter understands the situation or dilemma. Expressive managers experience tremendous highs and lows; participating in

the celebration of the good times is just as important as commiser-
ating during the bad.

A key aspect of the strategy involves protecting the expressive
managers' egos by supporting their positions and validating their
worth to others within and outside the sales group. One of the
biggest insults to any manager, and expressive ones in particular, is
being contradicted in public. Conversely, announcing their successes and broadcasting compliments will definitely yield relationship rewards.

Sergeants

The sergeant is named after the field sergeant in a military organization. Sergeants develop an intense loyalty to their team,
perhaps even greater than their personal loyalty to their company. They are hard workers who are constantly worrying about
their troops. They will even sacrifice their own best interests and
tolerate personal hardships if they feel these measures will benefit
their team.

Sergeants are likable, reliable people who have an intense
pride in their work. They have a humble demeanor and will un-
selfishly pass any praise they receive directly to the team. They
wear their emotions on their sleeves, and their team members always know where they stand. While they understand their place
in the organization and are confident of their own ability, they
still feel somewhat expendable and may suffer from self-doubt.
They do not accept criticism easily and will take faultfinding to
heart. However, sergeants are typically some of the last people to
leave a failing company and may have a history of staying with
companies long after the good times have passed.

The strategy for building a successful relationship with a sergeant is based on straightforward sincerity. Since sergeants are
"tell it like it is" people, Heavy Hitters' communications with
them are open, honest, and candid. For example, sergeants want

to know the bad news as soon as possible and don't appreciate it being sugarcoated.

Teflon Managers

Teflon managers are pleasant, agreeable, and polite people. However, unlike sergeants, you may never really get to know Teflon managers, even after working with them for years. They avoid disclosing personal information or give just enough to be thought of as friendly. From this standpoint, some people will consider them superficial. Another characteristic of Teflon managers is their ability to stay above the daily fray of politics. Yet while they seem cooperative, they are usually very stubborn when it comes to their personal agendas.

Regardless of the situation, Teflon managers are even-keeled and rarely frazzled. They always seem to be in control of their emotions and relate to others mainly in an edited, businesslike demeanor. You will not find these people yelling in the office, and they rarely socialize or develop personal friendships with coworkers. They will share their honest feelings only when there is little personal risk and if sharing this information benefits their business position.

Nothing sticks to Teflon managers. Bad news that would devastate sergeants or expressive managers bounces off them. Teflon managers just keep moving forward and never seem to be depressed or to give up. They enjoy prestige and title and act the part accordingly.

Working for Teflon managers creates an interesting dichotomy because of their personal nonattachment, comfort with solitude, idealized self-image, and desire to remain safe from criticism. Therefore, employ a "patient Pollyanna" strategy to dovetail with these Teflon manager characteristics. Exude a cheerful, pleasant disposition to communicate everything is okay, even under the most dire circumstances.

To help keep themselves immune to criticism, Heavy Hitters adopt a politically correct demeanor, rarely making cynical statements and repressing any open display of anger or disrespect to others. Patience and temperance are virtues Teflon managers appreciate.

Amateur Managers

Amateur managers are the toughest of all the types to work with. Whereas they may make a great first impression, analogous to a great first date, each subsequent date becomes more painful and frustrating. Amateur managers most likely do not have an extensive day-to-day background in sales, are very new to sales management, or lack the ability to manage a sales force.

Amateur managers fear being judged negatively by their superiors and peers, as well as their subordinates. Therefore, they may perceive the company as unfriendly or hostile. Their fears may also play an interesting part in their decision process. Under stress they become worried and indecisive or they propose so many different solutions that nothing ever happens. Or they may create outlandish plans and elaborate schemes that can't possibly be implemented in the real world. The mood of the sales department is schizophrenic and changes from moment to moment. Sometimes it is one of cheerful permissiveness, whereas other times the department is run with iron-fisted authority.

The strategy for working with amateur managers is opposite from the strategies for all of the other management styles. Instead of investing in and building the relationship, you actually search for a way to be released or escape from it. You seek a strategy for liberation from the amateur manager.

Several different methods can be used to be released from the relationship. Heavy Hitters could ask for a transfer or reassignment, seek a promotion, quit, or be fired. Each of these is perfectly acceptable. "Being fired is acceptable?" you may be asking yourself.

Absolutely. Heavy Hitters know time is short and do not want to waste their lives making incompetent people money. They want to surround themselves with successful people they respect. They have the confidence to stand up for themselves and what they believe in.

Micromanagers

Micromanagers are the most organized and methodical of all the management types. They have a strong sense of responsibility to their company, and they pride themselves on achieving their revenue goals. They tend to be black-and-white, all-or-nothing thinkers who want things done their way. They may have laboriously created methodical processes for every aspect of their jobs, most likely having used these same processes at previous companies.

Their endless stream of formal and informal regulations sometimes distracts salespeople from achieving results. They tend to hire people who they know will carry out their instructions to the letter, and even though one of the team members may achieve success, they will criticize that person if it wasn't done their way.

When working with micromanagers, adopt a long-term strategy based on their concept of the perfect performance of an efficient, industrious, and competent salesperson. Working efficiently equals being organized in the mind of a micromanager. Industriousness is akin to a singleminded, business-only attitude toward the job as evidenced by working long hours. A competent salesperson will complete tasks using the established processes. In addition, a constant flow of information is critical to ensure a smoothly functioning world; therefore, overcommunicate by staying in constant touch.

Overconfident Managers

Overconfident managers are on the opposite end of the humility spectrum from sergeants. They tend to be self-centered and self-absorbed. While charming and gregarious in public, they rarely have deep relationships in private. When they do take an active interest in developing a relationship, it is because they believe it will benefit their cause—having orchestrated strong relationships with their superiors.

Overconfident managers just love to talk about themselves and don't exhibit a great depth of feeling for others. They may boast of past successes and frequently recount stories about these achievements, regardless of whether someone may have heard them before. Not surprisingly, arrogance makes them susceptible to judgmental mistakes. They also enjoy being the life of the party and know how to make any party an unforgettable event. They are typically flashier dressers and very concerned with their appearance.

They will receive strong reactions when they participate in sales situations. Some customers will absolutely love them, while others will have an equally strong opposite reaction. Similarly, they will not relate equally well with all members of the team. Rather, they will have a few favorites who resemble them.

They are not open to feedback and are known to get quite defensive when criticized. They will get the job done their way and succeed at any cost. Although they are not exemplary planners, their sheer drive and tenacity make them well suited for roles where they have to launch a new product line or a new company.

Overconfident managers build a sales team of fighting gladiators who possess extraordinary willpower, mental toughness, animated spirit, and intelligence. To be included in this team, Heavy Hitters adopt the "clever conqueror" long-term strategy.

To be a conqueror, you must attack your enemies, be comfortable fighting for the cause, and be unafraid of rankling people in the process because the end justifies the means. You also cannot reveal any weakness, such as fear, self-doubt, sadness, or embarrassment. Only the attacker can be victorious; at best, the defender will merely survive.

Tip: The structure of a sales department will mirror the sales management style of its leader. Since leaders will naturally imprint themselves on their organizations, it is critical to understand what style of sales leader you work for. Do you work for an expressive manager? Is your manager equal parts mentor and overconfident manager? If you have a problem with your manager, consider these important points when determining why your relationship with your manager isn't working.

SIX COMMENTS

My wife subscribes to several women's magazines, so a few are always lying around the house. Whenever I glance at the covers, I invariably see articles with titles like "Ten Steps to a Happier Marriage" or "Seven Ways to Reignite Your Marriage." I always thought a more helpful article would be titled "Six Comments You Should Never Say to Your Spouse in Sales."

1. "Did you close the deal?" Of course, we appreciate your interest in our closing business because it directly affects our family's future, but we already have a very important person in our lives who asks us the same irritating question every day—our sales manager! Spouses play many different roles—friends, lovers, and caregivers—but they should never be sales managers.

2. "How did the big meeting go today?" The answer to this question is obvious. If we come home pumped up with adrenaline, the meeting went great and we will volunteer all the details from our award-winning performance earlier that day. If we don't say anything about it, don't ask! It will only remind us of how badly it went.

3. "If I were you, I would . . ." Maybe in a moment of self-doubt we'll open up to you about a particular deal we are working on. Even though we vent our worries and frustrations, we are not asking for advice. We are only seeking your empathy to our plight and reminding you how hard it is being in sales. Maybe deep down we also want you to be a little scared. Knowing the big commission check won't be coming may make you think twice before you spend money on things we don't need right now.

4. "Her husband is a doctor!" This backhanded insult shows us you really don't know what we do for a living. We work harder than many doctors, are more ethical than some lawyers, face fear like police officers, and are just as smart about the hard knocks of life as university professors. The future of our company, the livelihoods of all its employees and the welfare of their families, the vendors to whom our company owes money, and the dreams of our investors are all dependent upon our success.

5. "Why can't you stop thinking about work and relax?" Unlike other entitlement-based jobs, ours is based solely upon performance. We work in a Darwinian "survival of the fittest" environment. Someone is always waiting in the wings who would like to occupy our position as the top rep or to take our job. The strange part is that we are actually addicted to being in this state of perpetual competition. We enjoy the thrill of the hunt and the taste of the kill.

6. "Knock 'em dead, Tiger!" We don't want to hear a superficial rah-rah speech as if we were eight-year-olds at a Little League game. We are in the fight of our lives every day and would rather hear a heartfelt "I'll be thinking about you today."

Tip: Perhaps you know someone you should share this list with.

SELF-PERCEPTION

My secret pastime is reading Internet personal ads (but not for the reason you may be thinking). From a sales perspective, it is very interesting to see how people describe and explain what they are looking for in life in just a few sentences. Here are a few representative examples.

How to Sum Myself Up in a Few Words?
Easygoing, intelligent, sincere, honest, confident, loyal, sports fan, positive, thoughtful, romantic, career-oriented, passionate, loving, feminine, affectionate, good-looking, and vivacious.

If You Like John Goodman . . .
Some people I say I look like John Goodman and that I am a good man.

Angel Seeks Heaven on Earth . . . Smart, Sweet, Svelte, Sensual!
I am looking for someone who is first and foremost intelligent (I prefer the intellectual types), respectful, centered, successful (unpretentious), secure within themselves, honest, fit, adventurous, sophisticated, romantic, a great sense of humor, and someone who has a great sense of adventure since I love to travel!

Are You My God?
Sweep me off my feet, you sexy Roman god, and treat me like a goddess. Spoil me with romance and endless happiness. Stimulate my mind, caress my soul, and ignite my passion. You exceptional, stunning, hot, handsome hunk. I want it all.

Tina, Come Get Some Ham!
I know that movie is so silly and stupid, but I love it! If you don't know what movie I'm talking about, then we are not a good match.

Some people have misconceptions about themselves; they think they are perfect and can do no wrong. Some people are searching for perfection, which they'll never find. And some people are plain weird.

After interviewing hundreds of longtime salespeople who have enjoyed successful careers, I have found they all share three common characteristics. First, they truly enjoy people and love to be around them. Second, they don't take themselves too seriously. Finally, while they are passionate about success, they don't broadcast their passion aloud. They prove it with results.

Tip: The most impressive salespeople are the humblest ones.

FREEDOM

When people in other careers ask salespeople why they are in sales, the most frequent answer is "money." This is the pat answer salespeople give to outsiders who have never experienced the rush of closing a deal or the satisfaction of building a trusted friendship with a customer.

Providing the answer "money" is similar to the way mountain climbers answer "because it's there" when asked why they climb mountains. The questioners can't comprehend why someone would intentionally endure such physical and mental exhaustion and take such huge risks. They themselves don't possess the inward drive to reach the pinnacle or the self-confidence to attempt the impossible.

The real answer to the question of why salespeople are in sales is deeper and far more complex. It was best explained by French aristocrat and historian Alexis de Tocqueville when he wrote about the American colonies' desire to be free from England. "The revolution of the United States was the result of a mature reflecting preference for freedom, not a vague or ill-defined craving for independence," he concluded.[3] The colonials weren't as interested in the independence of the colonies as they were in the freedom of the individual. The writers of the Declaration of Independence considered freedom a natural law of nature.

Tip: The reality is that you are not in sales solely for money. You work in sales not because you have to but because you have to be free. And this fundamental drive is at the core of the human spirit.

SHARPSHOOTER

In eleventh-century England, King William was making preparations to go hunting in the forest. As he was getting ready with his attendants, six exquisitely crafted arrows were presented to him. After praising their craftsmanship, he kept four for himself and handed two to the knight of Poix. "It is only right," he said, "that the sharpest should be given to the man who knows how to shoot the deadliest shots."[4]

Usually, it is a very difficult judgment call for a manager to reassign an important account from one salesperson to another. Whether the change is initiated by the manager or requested by another salesperson or even the customer, some circumstances demand that a change be made for the greater good of the company. When faced with such a circumstance, all parties involved must act with gracious magnanimity, rising above pettiness and overlooking insult.

Tip: Of course, sales is an "every man for himself" profession, and salespeople who fight for what they believe in deserve respect. However, at times, in order for the team as a whole to survive, everyone in the lifeboat must relinquish their self-centered aspirations and row in the same direction.

FATAL FAUX PAS

Since salespeople talk day in and day out, it's not surprising that we make faux pas. Other times, we do things that are just plain stupid. Here are a few of my favorite bloopers.

A salesperson scheduled a lunchtime demonstration in a customer's conference room and had sandwiches brought in for the attendees. Plenty of food was left over, so as the demonstration wound down, other employees were invited in to help themselves. One by one, people came in and grabbed a sandwich and some of the other food while the salesperson and the attendees made small talk. A plump woman walked in and started filling her plate, whereupon the salesperson remarked, "Take all you want since you are eating for two." However, the woman wasn't pregnant. The room fell silent and the woman glared at the salesperson: "What did you say?" The salesperson fumbled for an answer but couldn't find one. The woman stormed out of the room and everyone else sheepishly walked out, leaving the salesperson alone in his humiliation.

A salesperson and his presales engineer had been clowning around with the PowerPoint presentation they gave to customers. They had a good laugh together as they changed the slides and made fun of their company and its products. However, the fun was short-lived: When they gave the presentation the next day to a new account, the third slide said, "Our products stink and you really shouldn't buy them."

After a long day of meetings at a company sales kickoff, the salespeople retired to the hotel bar for drinks. The bar for this particular hotel was in the atrium, where drinkers could watch hotel guests in the glass-encased elevators go up and down. By early evening, it was quite apparent that one salesman had had too much drink. Barely able to talk coherently, he staggered to the elevator and passed out on the floor. Everyone in the bar laughed while he rode the elevator up and down—until the vice president of sales saw what was happening and had him loaded on a bellman's cart and hauled to his room.

A sales rep I worked with posted his 67-cent monthly commission check on his cubicle wall. I laughed every time I saw it. But I never understood the man who hung a boudoir photo of his wife in his office. Right behind his desk was a revealing picture of his lingerie-clad wife. While he thought it was special and it made him feel like a big man, everyone else thought it was bizarre and wondered why he would want colleagues and strangers leering at his wife all day.

Tip: You are constantly being judged by your peers and management. How seriously do you take your job? How do you behave at sales meetings? And what's on your workplace walls?

FACING THE END

General George Patton was in deep trouble. During a visit to a hospital full of wounded GIs in Sicily, he had slapped a soldier suffering from battle fatigue and accused him of cowardice. The reports of the incident caused a public outcry back in the States, and Congress demanded his resignation. Patton's diary entry on May 1, 1944, about his meeting with his commander, Dwight D. Eisenhower, reveals his innermost thoughts.

> In spite of possible execution this morning I slept well and trust my destiny. God has never let me, or the country,

down yet. Reported to Ike at 1100. He was most cordial and asked me to sit down, so I felt a little reassured. He said, "George, you have gotten yourself into a very serious fix." I said, "Before you go any farther, I want to say that your job is more important than mine, so if in trying to save me you are hurting yourself, throw me out." . . . He went on to say that General Marshall had wired him that my repeated mistakes have shaken the confidence of the country and the War Department. . . .

. . . Ike said General Marshall had told him that my crime had destroyed all chance of my permanent promotion, as the opposition said even if I was the best tactician and strategist in the army, my demonstrated lack of judgment made me unfit to command. He said that he had wired General Marshall on Sunday washing his hands of me. (He did not use these words but that is what he meant.) . . .

. . . When I came out I don't think anyone could tell that I had just been killed. I have lost lots of competitions in the sporting way, but I never did better. I feel like death, but I am not out yet. If they will let me fight, I will; but if not, I will resign so as to be able to talk, and then I will tell the truth, and possibly do my country more good. All the way home, 5 hours, I recited poetry to myself.

> *If you can make a heap of all your winnings*
> *And risk them on one game of pitch and toss*
> *And lose, and start at your beginning*
> *And never breathe a word about your loss.*[5]

The ending of any sales job is never pretty. Even a salesperson who has faithfully served his company for years is usually shown the door as soon as he turns in his two weeks' notice. In the high-tech industry, where I have spent my career, vice presidents have an average tenure of only 18 months. They are usually fired to protect the reputations of others.

Tip: At some point during your career, you will most likely find yourself in an untenable position where you are fired or have to resign. Usually, it is an issue of your fit with the job rather than your ability to do the job. So if you are giving 100 percent of your heart and soul to your company, hold a little piece back in anticipation of the end. Remember, failure must occur for success to exist.

KEEP YOUR GOALS TO YOURSELF

No one wants to be around braggarts who constantly remind everyone of their sales prowess. Even worse are salespeople who continue to talk about the big deals they will close although their track record indicates that few, if any, will actually come through. This comment from the sports section of my local newspaper tells an important lesson.

> Here is a lesson I am sure Annika Sorenstam learned this weekend: Keep your goals to yourself. The world's greatest player at the moment, male or female, boldly announced that she wanted to win all four major championships this year. It's not like she couldn't do it. She won two of four last year and finished second and fourth in the other two.
>
> But at last week's Kraft Nabisco Championship, the first major event of this year, her quest was over after the second round. She struggled under the pressure of the announcement in the first two rounds and couldn't recover, despite shooting 69s on Saturday and Sunday. Now the only Grand Slam she is getting is if she orders it from Denny's. This won't affect her golf, but it might make her more reserved in the future.[6]

Tip: An old sports adage applies equally to sales: "Never have your victory party before you have your victory."

PRECONCEIVED IDEAS

My friend Larry had been summoned for jury duty. Since it would take him away from the business he ran, he was none too happy about it. The pool of one hundred potential jurors was assembled at the downtown courthouse, and the prosecuting and defending attorneys began their interviews to select those who would decide a felony case.

All of the potential jurors listened to the questions being asked by the attorneys as each person was interviewed. The attorneys were trying to understand each individual's background and ascertain biases that might affect their ability to win the case. Larry snobbishly said that he could not believe the ignorance he perceived in most of the answers the prospective jurors gave. He told me he felt this most certainly was not going to be a jury made up of his peers.

The prosecuting attorney from the district attorney's office had set up a large picture on an easel. It was a picture of an elephant. However, it showed only the trunk, tail, feet, shoulder, and hindquarters. The entire middle section of the elephant was missing. Maybe because she was missing some important piece of evidence in her case, the DA was trying to find out if the jurors would conclude it was an elephant from only a subset of information. It also seemed to Larry she was grandstanding a bit. Larry silently told himself, *It's a damn elephant. Can't we just get this over with?*

The next person interviewed on the stand was a 70-year-old woman. She was asked what she thought about the elephant picture. She gave the most eloquent explanation about how she had once seen an elephant picture very similar to that one. In the middle, missing section was a man holding up an elephant costume. Larry recalled that it was so quiet at that moment you could have heard a pin drop. The district attorney's reaction said it all. She was dumbfounded and didn't know what to say. The woman was right. The DA's picture could have easily been the picture she described.

The illustration the DA thought would help her make a key point actually worked against her case and damaged her credibility. Larry said he was absolutely humbled by the prospective juror's words. He had jumped to the wrong conclusion about the picture and had completely misjudged the other jurors in the courtroom that day.

Tip: Reading people correctly is a mandatory ability for salespeople who want to enjoy long careers. Being able to ascertain a customer's power and influence is absolutely necessary. It is human nature for salespeople who have made hundreds of sales calls to start stereotyping people's importance. However, every decision maker's role in the sales cycle is as unique as his or her personality. You will end up being wrong more often than you are right when you make broad generalizations about customers.

HEY, HEY, WE'RE THE MONKEYS

Nineteenth-century scientist Thomas Huxley introduced the mathematical notion that monkeys typing at random will eventually produce the works of Shakespeare. To test this theory, a few years ago researchers at Plymouth University in England put six Sulawesi crested macaques in a room with a computer and keyboards for four weeks.

At first, the lead male picked up a stone and started "bashing the hell out of the computer," according to researcher Mike

Phillips. "Another thing they were interested in was defecating and urinating all over the keyboard," he said.[7]

Over the course of a month, monkeys Elmo, Gum, Heather, Holly, Mistletoe, and Rowan did not make even a single literate word. By the experiment's end, they had produced five pages of text consisting mainly of *S*s and the letters *A*, *J*, *L*, and *M*. The monkeys simply did not have the intelligence and wherewithal to succeed.

Tip: What's your sales environment like? Do you respect your peers and admire your managers? When you feel like you're working with a bunch of monkeys, it's time to move on.

MONDAY-MORNING QUARTERBACKS

You may have read in your history books that Peter Minuit of the Dutch West India Company bought Manhattan Island from the Indians for $24. However, you probably didn't know that he was fined for doing so on a charge of extravagance. This situation reminds me of the salesperson who, after performing a minor miracle, won an extremely competitive deal. When he brought the deal back to the office, he was greeted not with congratulations but with criticisms.

As the order passed from the jurisdiction of one company sovereignty to another, all the handlers felt compelled to offer their two cents' worth of demotivating comments. The salesperson's manager told him that he could have done better. The accounting supervisor was hesitant to accept the order because the discount was a few points above average. The legal counselor questioned some inconsequential language on the back of the purchase order. The order entry clerk complained that the forms weren't filled out to her standard of perfection. The sales compensation manager argued the salesperson should receive less than the normal credit because of the excessive discount. All of these Monday-morning quarterbacks had forgotten one important fact: The salesperson came through with a great win that enabled the company to continue paying them for doing their jobs. In this regard, salespeople have the most important job in the company.

Tip: Tell the Monday-morning quarterbacks that every company's most important assets are its customers and that salespeople are the ones who are tasked with the vital responsibility of recruiting and keeping them.

SO YOU WANT TO BE A MANAGER

Salespeople want to move into management for many different reasons. Some want their careers to progress to the next logical step. Others feel they can make an impact on their organization through the knowledge they have accumulated. And some are tired of being on the front line and want to move into what they consider a less stressful position. However, most salespeople underestimate the complexity of the role, as evidenced by this story from a sales manager friend of mine.

A salesperson had scheduled an introductory meeting with his newly named manager. As the meeting began, they made casual conversation for a few minutes about the nature of sales. Then the salesperson volunteered some somewhat shocking information about his lifestyle. Caught off guard, the manager asked him if he really wanted to talk about this very private subject. The salesman answered, "Sure." Next, he dropped an atom bomb of information in the manager's lap about his personal torment over this situation.

Two more times the manager asked him whether he really wanted to chat about such a deeply personal topic. The salesperson responded yes each time. The new manager really didn't want to talk about it but didn't know what to do. He tried to change the subject, but the salesperson kept bringing the conversation back to his personal situation. Although the manager was sympathetic to the salesperson's plight, he could not condone his actions, and the conversation ended awkwardly.

Two days later, the manager received a message from the vice president. The salesperson had complained to him that he thought their topic of conversation was inappropriate. The vice president asked the salesperson and manager to meet and clear up the matter.

Their meeting started with the manager telling the salesperson how sorry he was that the salesperson thought their conversation was negative. He reminded the salesperson that on several occasions he had asked if the salesperson truly wanted to continue on the personal subject and each time he had said yes. The salesperson acknowledged this and then gave the real reason for his complaint: "Well, you need to do some damage control."

Here's the interesting part. It wasn't the manager who needed to do the damage control. It was actually the embarrassed salesperson. He had revealed some private information about himself that he had never told another coworker. Afterward, he probably had second thoughts about telling his new boss—a complete stranger—about skeletons he wished had remained hidden in his closet. He decided that the only way to cover his own tracks was to discredit the manager, even though the salesperson was the one who made the mistake of sharing personal information that was inappropriate for the workplace.

Tip: Whether you are a manager or a salesperson, you must maintain a line between your work and your personal life. Wherever the imaginary boundary between work and private life is crossed, the misstep will most likely come back to haunt everyone involved.

LOST CAUSE

In December 1944, Japanese intelligence officer Lieutenant Hiroo Onoda was ordered to the Philippine island of Lubang. His mission was to gather reconnaissance information and conduct guerrilla warfare. His orders were very specific: Under no circumstance was he to surrender or to take his life with his own hand. It might take months or years, but the army would come back for him.

Onoda took these orders literally and spent the next 29 years fighting a war that was over. He lived in the jungle, evaded search parties, and harassed villagers whenever possible. Over the course of the years, leaflets, letters, and family pictures were dropped urging his surrender. Onoda ignored them all.

It wasn't until 1974 that Onoda finally returned to Japan. A Japanese college dropout, Norio Suzuki, traveled to the Philippines to search for Onoda. When he found him, he tried to convince him the war was over, but Onoda said he would be convinced only if his commander ordered it. Suzuki returned with Onoda's former commander, who finally convinced him that he could end his mission. After he returned to Japan, Onoda wrote of the moment in his memoirs: "We really lost the war! . . . Suddenly everything went black. A storm raged inside me. I felt like a fool for having been so tense and cautious on the way here. Worse than that, what had I been doing for all these years?"[8]

Tip: Some salespeople ignore the truth about the predicament they're in and continue to labor in the jungles of lost-cause companies. They waste the best years of their careers in dead-end jobs, long after friends and colleagues have left for greener pastures. Learn to recognize lost causes and dead ends.

MISSING HISTORY

As the commuter flight took off from Southern California and headed to the Bay Area, the captain announced we were in for a real treat: We would have a bird's-eye view of an experimental test flight of a scram jet. He went on to explain that scram jets will someday replace all the jets used on aircraft today. He said that the flight time from Los Angeles to Tokyo will be reduced from 14 hours to 2 hours.

The unmanned scram jet had been loaded beneath a B-52 bomber to be released just off the Pacific coast. We could clearly see the vapor trail of the B-52 as it headed over the ocean. At 13,000 feet we could see a small puff of white smoke from underneath the B-52 and the scram jet rocketed at a 45-degree angle toward outer space. The passengers let out oohs and ahs at its incredible speed as it climbed to 40,000 feet. It would reach 7,000 miles per hour, or Mach 9.8, and set a new record for the fastest air-breathing aircraft ever to fly.[9] (The average commercial jet flies about 400 miles per hour.)

Since the commuter flight was less than half full, plenty of empty window seats were available on the left side of the airplane so that everyone could watch history in the making. Surprisingly, only a few passengers, including me, bothered to move. The others were too busy working on their laptops or too preoccupied with their reading materials to take the time to preview how their children's children would travel in the future. Frankly, I couldn't believe it. What could be so important that they would miss such an opportunity?

Tip: Sometimes you need to stop and smell the roses. As the saying goes, "The journey is the destination."

YOU'RE ALREADY RICH

I had an interesting conversation with a longtime salesperson at a party. In his own words, he had "carried the bag" for almost 30 years. At one point during his career, he tried a stint in sales management, but he didn't like it. He said that he "couldn't stand kowtowing to the big shots and couldn't take the whining from below." In my mind, he didn't seem to have much enthusiasm for selling, either.

As he was in his early 60s, I asked him if he was planning to retire soon. That's when the fellow, who owned a multimillion-dollar home and a new Porsche, responded by asking me if I thought he was rich or something. His comment led me to find some surprising information:

- Some 1.3 billion people live on less than a dollar a day.

- Three billion people, half the world's population, live on less than two dollars a day.

- Three billion people have no access to sanitation, and two billion have no access to electricity.[10]

From these facts, I drew the following conclusion: If you own a refrigerator, you are already richer than 95 percent of the world's population.

Tip: In your never-ending pursuit of financial nirvana, do not forget how blessed you already are.

FINAL ADVICE

The most important lesson I learned from all my years in sales is to live in the moment, not too focused on the past or transfixed by the future. Circumstances change very quickly in sales. You may have been a hero last quarter, but next quarter you start back at zero. The funnel of deals you may have been counting on for months could disappear in a few minutes. The company whose account you worked so hard to close may want its money back because the product isn't working right. Your new sales manager may turn out to be your worst nightmare. Every salesperson knows this profession provides no guarantees, and fate can be very fickle indeed.

So here's my final advice about your sales career. Treasure all the moments: the good and the bad. Always keep your sense of humor. Remember, you are very fortunate to be in sales. It is one of the few professions in which you have the opportunity to bond through battle and to create and conquer on a daily basis. Most importantly, you have been given the chance to build relationships with colleagues and customers every day. Never forget, the company you work for is not nearly as important as the people you work with. It is through your relationships that you leave your mark on the world.

Epilogue

History can tell us so much about the present if we choose to listen. In closing, I'd like to share a few of my favorite quotes from Sun Tzu, Napoleon Bonaparte, George Patton, Buddha, Jesus Christ, and Ronald Reagan.

> To secure ourselves against defeat lies in our hands, but the opportunity to defeat the enemy is provided by the enemy himself.[1]

I have met many talented salespeople throughout my career. They came from all walks of life and sold in very different ways. What they all had in common, though, was the ability to naturally find a way to win. They knew how to maximize their strengths and minimize their weaknesses, the essence of the indirect strategy.

In order to win, we must make our opponents lose. In professional tennis, the average point is decided in less than two strokes. The winner hits shots the opponent doesn't like to places on the court the opponent can't reach. The same strategy applies to sales.

> There are two levers for moving men: interest and fear.[2]

I have reiterated throughout the book that the customer's human nature is what ultimately determines the winner for one reason and one reason only—it is the absolute truth! However, most salespeople find the human element of selling to be hard to predict and difficult to manage, so they fall back on the logical selling of product features and functions. Always remember, think people first, products second.

> If we take the generally accepted definition of bravery as a quality that knows not fear, I have never seen a brave man. All men are frightened. The more intelligent they are, the more they are frightened. The courageous man is the man who forces himself, in spite of his fear, to carry on.[3]

It's healthy for salespeople to always be on edge and wonder what they don't know about the deals they're working on. Heavy Hitters don't repress their worries and hope everything will work out. They set about trying to find answers and information to satisfy their curiosity. The courageous salesperson faces his fears in the never-ending pursuit of the ultimate truth, "Will I win the deal?"

> It is easy to shield the outer body from poisoned arrows, but it is impossible to shield the mind from the poisoned darts that originate within oneself.[4]

The true enemies of every salesperson are depression, hopelessness, and loss of confidence. It seems that learning to be happy with oneself takes a lifetime to achieve. In the meantime, don't be so hard on yourself.

> If a village won't welcome you or listen to you, shake the dust from your feet as you leave.[5]

The secret of sales, as well as of life, is turning failure into success, being able to not only learn from your mistakes but make the best of bad situations. You've probably already run into your share of closed-minded customers who have treated you shabbily. The most important qualification criterion in any account, far greater than business and technical fit, is whether it is a place where you can be "loved." In other words, does it provide a situation where you have the potential to develop close personal relationships? In reality, nothing else matters.

> Our sons and daughters will in their lifetime undoubtedly see things almost impossible for us to imagine. But in my opinion the generation to which I belong will have had an experience they will not know.[6]

I highly doubt any of my children will wind up in sales. Sales is not like a family-owned business that's passed down from generation to generation. Nor is it like politics, where family members can ride the coattails of a patriarch to power. Rather, we have chosen the sales profession to provide a better future for our families. Our sacrifice—the long hours, pressure to perform, and endless worry—is made to provide them the freedom to live their lives as they choose.

We want to be thought of as the hero who was able to make the family's dreams come true. We seek to provide them an idyllic lifestyle, and we want those we love to live in comfort, if not luxury. We want our children to attend the best schools and enjoy fruitful careers doing what they love. However, I feel some sadness that they will never experience the spirit of a sales career: the camaraderie, the drama of competition, the thrill of victory, and the agony of defeat. These life lessons are inherent to a career in sales.

Whether because of a calculated career move or by happenstance, you are in sales because you're supposed to be. In one sense, it wasn't even your decision. You are simply fulfilling your destiny. And in the words of philosopher José Ortega y Gasset, "Every living creature is happy when he fulfills his destiny, that is, when he realizes himself, when he is being that which in truth he is."[7]

I'd like to end the book with an excerpt from a poem written by 17-year-old Ronald Reagan long before he knew what fate had in store for him.

> *Millions have gone before us,*
> *And millions will come behind.*
> *So why do we curse and fight*
> *At a fate both wise and kind.*[8]

May your future be filled with greatness, and may you reach the final destination of success.

Notes

Introduction

1. Martin Blumenson, *Patton: Man behind the Legend* (New York: William Morrow, 1985), 296.
2. Donald Lambro and Ralph Z. Hallow, "History Embraces Reagan's Legacy," *Washington Times*, June 12, 2004, http://www.washtimes.com/national/20040612-120318-7155r.htm (accessed June 1, 2005).
3. *Webster's New World College Dictionary*, 3rd ed., ed. Victoria Neufeldt (New York: Prentice Hall, 1996), s.v. "wisdom."

Chapter 1   The Grand Strategy of War

1. Richard Rollins, "Lee's Artillery Prepares for Picket's Charge," Battery B, 4th U.S. Light Artillery, http://www.batteryb.com/pickets_charge_artillery.html (accessed June 3, 2005).
2. Ibid.
3. Ferndale School, "Pickett's Charge," http://home.cinci.rr.com/morins/page4.html (accessed May 25, 2005).
4. Gettysburg National Military Park, "The Fame of Pickett's Charge," National Park Service, http://www.nps.gov/gett/getttour/sidebar/pickett.htm (accessed June 4, 2005).
5. Peter Lyman and Hal R. Varian, "How Much Information?" University of California at Berkeley, http://www.sims.berkeley.edu/research/projects/how-much-info/ (accessed May 22, 2005).
6. *USA Today*, "Media Kit," http://www.usatoday.com/media_kit/usatoday/ut_usatoday_home.htm?POE=FOOTER (accessed June 3, 2005).
7. B. H. Liddell Hart, *Strategy* (New York: Frederick A. Praeger, 1954), 18.
8. Ibid.
9. Ibid.
10. Ibid.
11. Sun Tzu, *The Art of War*, ed. James Clavell (New York: Delacorte Press, 1983), 21.
12. Ibid., 20.
13. Napoleonic Guide, "Maxims of Napoleon Bonaparte," http://www.napoleonguide.com/maxim_war.htm (accessed June 6, 2005).

14. Liddell Hart, *Strategy*, 1.
15. George S. Patton, *War as I Knew It* (Boston: Houghton Mifflin, 1995), xiv.
16. Alexander Moseley, "The Philosophy of War," *Internet Encyclopedia of Philosophy*, http://www.iep.utm.edu/w/war.htm (accessed June 13, 2005).
17. Sun Tzu, *Art of War*, 15.
18. Napoleonic Guide, "Maxims of Napoleon Bonaparte."
19. Robert Nightengale, "Little Bighorn Cover Up," About.com, http://americanhistory.about.com/library/prm/bllittlebighorn1.htm?terms=custer (accessed June 1, 2005).
20. Napoleonic Guide, "Maxims of Napoleon Bonaparte."
21. Dave Ostrander, "World War II Radio Communications," http://www.labradorman.com/Reenacting/Research/WW2_Communications.htm (accessed June 14, 2005).
22. Henry Shorreck, "The Role of COMINT in the Battle of Midway," Ibiblio, http://www.ibiblio.org/hyperwar/PTO/Magic/COMINT-Midway.html (accessed June 12, 2005).
23. Sun Tzu, *Art of War*, 78.
24. Cedar Hill School, "Revolutionary War Quotes," Bernards Township School District, http://www.bernardsboe.com/Cedar-Hill/Linked-pages /Grade4/warquotes.htm (accessed June 22, 2005).
25. Liddell Hart, *Strategy*, 14.
26. Sun Tzu, *Art of War*, 11.
27. Liddell Hart, *Strategy*, 117.
28. "Military Quotes," Military-quotes.com, http://www.military-quotes.com/ Patton.htm (accessed June 3, 2005).
29. Harlan Ullman, *Shock and Awe: Achieving Rapid Dominance* (Whitefish, MT: Kessinger Publishing, 2004).
30. Patton, *War as I Knew It*, 405.
31. Liddell Hart, *Strategy*, 14.
32. Sun Tzu, *Art of War*, 11.
33. Napoleonic Guide, "Maxims of Napoleon Bonaparte."
34. John Omicinski, "Tet Offensive: A Turning Point," Vets with a Mission, http://www.vwam.com/vets/tet/turningpoint.html (accessed June 12, 2005).
35. Napoleonic Guide, "Maxims of Napoleon Bonaparte."
36. "Military Quotes," Military-quotes.com.
37. Henry Michaels, "US Plans 'Shock and Awe' Blitzkrieg in Iraq," World Socialist Web Site, http://www.wsws.org/articles/2003/jan2003/war-j30.shtml (accessed June 20, 2005).
38. Patton, *War as I Knew It*, 405.
39. Liddell Hart, *Strategy*, 25.
40. Sun Tzu, *Art of War*, 25.

Chapter 2   Battlefield Tactics

1. George Patton, "Patton's Famous Speech," The Patton Society, http://www.pattonhq.com/speech.html (accessed July 1, 2005).
2. Ibid.

3. Napoleonic Guide, "Maxims of Napoleon Bonaparte."

4. *Merriam-Webster Dictionary*, s.v. "reconnoiter," http://www.m-w.com/dictionary/reconnoiter (accessed June 14, 2005).

5. *United States Department of Defense Dictionary*, s.v. "Coup De Main," http://www.dtic.mil/doctrine/jel/doddict/data/c/01369.html (accessed June 12, 2005).

6. Dennis Connole, "A Bloody Encounter North of Rome," *World War II* Magazine, September 2003, 34.

7. Devildogg Country, "Gunnery Sgt. Carlos N. Hathcock II," http://www.geocities.com/devildogg4ever/allpages/carlos.html (accessed July 7, 2005).

8. Jon S. Powell, "Airland Battle: The Wrong Doctrine for the Wrong Reason," Air University Review, http://www.airpower.maxwell.af.mil/airchronicles/aureview/1985/may-jun/powell.html (accessed July 24, 2005).

9. Charles Jones, "Into the Meat Grinder," *World War II* Magazine, March 2005, 46.

10. Jim Noonan, e-mail message to author, March 7, 2005.

11. B. H. Liddell Hart, *Strategy* (New York: Frederick A. Praeger, 1954), 13.

Chapter 3   The Five Steps to Victory

1. Sun Tzu, *The Art of War*, ed. James Clavell (New York: Delacorte Press, 1983), 45.

2. Napoleonic Guide, "Maxims of Napoleon Bonaparte" (accessed August 4, 2005).

3. Ibid.

4. Atozquotes, "George S. Patton," http://www.atozquotes.com/author.asp?author=George+S.+Patton (accessed January 4, 2006).

5. Napoleonic Guide, "Maxims of Napoleon Bonaparte."

6. Sun Tzu, *Art of War*, 81.

7. Ibid., 2.

Chapter 4   Real Persuasion

1. Mark Sherman, "Obesity May Pass Smoking as Top Killer," Associated Press, http://www.stopgettingsick.com/templates/news_template.cfm/7423.

2. Ibid.

3. Dayana Yochim, "What's in Your Purse?" The Motley Fool, http://creditcardnation.com/motleyfool111803.html (accessed March 7, 2004).

4. Reuters, "Americans Struggle with Credit Card Bills," Yahoo!, http://story.news.com/20040305/bs_nm/financial_creditcards_dc_2 (accessed March 5, 2004).

5. Society for the Promotion of Buddhism, *The Teaching of Buddha* (Tokyo: Kosaido Printing Co., 1995), 106.

6. Ibid., 64.

7. Greg Laurie, ed., *New Believer's Bible* (Wheaton, IL: Tyndale, 1996), Luke 6:24–25.

8. Society for the Promotion of Buddhism, *Teaching of Buddha*, 28.

9. Jim Hallowes and Amy Hallowes, "Being Highly Sensitive," About.com, http://healing.about.com/od/empathic/a/HSP_hallowes.htm (accessed September 3, 2005).

10. Society for the Promotion of Buddhism, *Teaching of Buddha*, 104.

11. Ronald Reagan, "Tear Down This Wall," The Reagan Foundation, http://www.reaganfoundation.org/reagan/speeches/wall.asp (accessed July 4, 2005).

12. Ronald Reagan, *Reagan, in His Own Hand: The Writings of Ronald Reagan That Reveal His Revolutionary Vision for America*, ed. Kiron K. Skinner, Annelise Anderson, and Martin Anderson (New York: Free Press, 2001), 10.

13. George P. Shultz, Foreword to *Reagan, in His Own Hand: The Writings of Ronald Reagan That Reveal His Revolutionary Vision for America*, ed. Kiron K. Skinner, Annelise Anderson, and Martin Anderson (New York: Free Press, 2001), xii.

14. Reagan, *Reagan, in His Own Hand*, 421.

15. Society for the Promotion of Buddhism, *Teaching of Buddha*, 24.

16. Ibid., 4.

17. Ibid., 8.

18. Laurie, *New Believer's Bible*, John 14:6.

19. Reagan, "Tear Down This Wall."

20. Laurie, *New Believer's Bible*, Matt. 19:24.

21. Society for the Promotion of Buddhism, *Teaching of Buddha*, 306.

22. Ronald Reagan, "Ronald Reagan Quotes," Brainy Quote, http://www.brainyquote.com/quotes/authors/r/ronald_reagan.html (accessed July 23, 2005).

23. *Dream Homes* Magazine, vol. 53, 2005.

24. Eugene Peterson, ed., *The Message* (Colorado Springs: Navpress, 1993), Matt. 13:13.

25. Society for the Promotion of Buddhism, *Teaching of Buddha*, 148.

26. Ibid., 58.

27. Laurie, *New Believer's Bible*, John 4:4–30.

28. CBS News, "Ronald Reagan, Master Storyteller," *48 Hours*, June 7, 2004, http://www.cbsnews.com/stories/2004/06/07/48hours/main621459.shtml (accessed July 25, 2005).

29. Daniel Kurtzman, "Funny Quotes by President Reagan," About.com, http://politicalhumor.about.com/cs/quotethis/a/reaganquotes.htm (accessed July 25, 2005).

30. Ronald Reagan, "Quote Details: Ronald Reagan," The Quotations Page, http://www.quotationspage.com/quote/325.html (accessed July 26, 2005).

31. Ibid.

32. Ward Fredricks, "It's a Great Story," The Phrase Finder, http://www.phrases.org.uk/bulletin_board/28/messages/718.html (accessed July 26, 2005).

33. CBS News, "Ronald Reagan, Master Storyteller."

34. Society for the Promotion of Buddhism, *Teaching of Buddha*, 36.

35. Laurie, *New Believer's Bible*, Matt. 13:13.

36. Peggy Noonan, "Remember the Reagan Years," *National Review*, http://www.nationalreview.com/interrogatory/interrogatory020602.shtml (accessed July 26, 2005).

Chapter 5   Meeting of the Minds

1. David Partenheimer, "What Makes a Good President?" American Psychological Association, http://www.apa.org/releases/presidents.html (accessed August 13, 2005).

2. Michael Medved, "Four Ways to Measure the Presidency," *USA Today*, http://www.usatoday.com/news/opinion/editorials/2003-01-27-communication_x.htm (accessed August 14, 2005).

3. George Will, "A Poverty of Modern Thinking," *Orange County Register*, March 5, 2005.
4. Society for the Promotion of Buddhism, *The Teaching of Buddha* (Tokyo: Kosaido Printing Co., 1995), 160.
5. Claudia Parsons, "Study Shows U.S. Election Coverage Harder on Bush," Yahoo!, http://story.news.yahoo.com/news?tmpl=story&cid=564&ncid=564&e=2&u=/nm/20050314/ts_nm/media_report_dc (accessed August 14, 2005).
6. Doug Gamble, "Reagan's Message: Savor Our Freedoms," *Orange County Register*, July 4, 2005.

Chapter 6 Common-Sense Selling

1. Society for the Promotion of Buddhism, *The Teaching of Buddha* (Tokyo: Kosaido Printing Co., 1995), 228.
2. Seventy-First Congress, "Battle of Camden," U.S. Army Center of Military History, http://www.army.mil/Cmh-Pg/books/RevWar/Camden/AWC-CAM2.htm#THEBATTLEOFCAMDEN (accessed August 4, 2005).
3. George S. Patton, *War as I Knew It* (Boston: Houghton Mifflin, 1995), 402.
4. Ely Portillo, "Passenger's Gender Can Make a Difference in Teen Driving," Yahoo!, http://news.yahoo.com/s/krwashbureau/20050826/ts_krwashbureau/_bc_teendrivers_wa (accessed August 21, 2005).
5. Sun Tzu, *The Art of War*, ed. James Clavell (New York: Delacorte Press, 1983), 2.
6. Gourmandizer e-zine, "James 'Diamond Jim' Brady," http://www.gourmandizer.com/ezine/brady/ (accessed August 1, 2005).
7. "Coaching Quotes," Fantasy Football Bookmarks, http://www.ffbookmarks.com/coaching_quotes.htm (accessed September 2, 2005).
8. Loel Schrader, " 'Old Coach' Steals the Show at Luncheon," University of Southern California, http://usctrojans.collegesports.com/sports/m-footbl/spec-rel/schrader-colm19.html (accessed August 22, 2005).
9. Ibid
10. John Whicker, "John Whicker's Column," *Orange County Register*, December 3, 2004.
11. Todd Harmonson, "History in the Making," *Orange County Register*, August 28, 2005.
12. National Commission on Terrorist Attacks, *9/11 Commission Report* (New York: W. W. Norton, 2004), 387.
13. "Boy, Were They Wrong!" Netscape, http://channels.netscape.com/ns/atplay/predictions.jsp (accessed September 4, 2005).
14. Ibid.
15. Henry Neils, "Avoiding Burnout," Microsoft News Network, http://msn.careerbuilder.com/Custom/MSN/CareerAdvice/WPI_AvoidingBurnout.htm?sc_extcmp=JS_wi09_dec03_home1&GT1=6396&cbRecursionCnt=1&cbsid=efa41cdfbd0e4b5fa19aad092777edba-168178476-r4-1 (accessed August 2, 2005).

Chapter 7 The Life of a Salesperson

1. Embassy of France, "History of the Creation of the Legion of Honor," http://www.info-france-usa.org/news/statmnts/1998/80ww1/histoire.asp (accessed September 11, 2005).

2. Society for the Promotion of Buddhism, *The Teaching of Buddha* (Tokyo: Kosaido Printing Co., 1995), 103.
3. Gary Galles, "De Tocqueville's Words Resound," *Orange County Register*, July 29, 2005.
4. Elizabeth Longford, *Oxford Book of Royal Anecdotes* (New York: Oxford University Press, 1989).
5. Library of Congress, "Churchill and the Great Republic," http://www.loc.gov/exhibits/churchill/wc-trans215.html (accessed July 14, 2005).
6. John Reger, "Keep Goals to Thyself," *Orange County Register*, April 1, 2005.
7. Jill Lawless, "Six Monkeys on Computer Create Only a Mess," *Orange County Register*, May 10, 2003.
8. Hiroo Onoda, *No Surrender: My Thirty-Year War*, trans. Charles S. Terry (New York: Kodansha International Ltd., 1974), 14.
9. "Boeing X43," Wikipedia, http://en.wikipedia.org/wiki/X-43A (accessed September 4, 2005).
10. Anup Shah, "Causes of Poverty," Global Issues Organization, http://www.globalissues.org/TradeRelated/Facts.asp (accessed September 22, 2005).

Epilogue

1. Sun Tzu, *The Art of War*, ed. James Clavell (New York: Delacorte Press, 1983), 19.
2. "Famous Quotes by Napoleon Bonaparte," Zaadz, http://www.zaadz.com/quotes/authors/napoleon_bonaparte?page=3 (accessed July 13, 2005).
3. George S. Patton, *War as I Knew It* (Boston: Houghton Mifflin, 1995), 340.
4. Society for the Promotion of Buddhism, *The Teaching of Buddha* (Tokyo: Kosaido Printing Co., 1995), 170.
5. Greg Laurie, ed., *New Believer's Bible* (Wheaton, IL: Tyndale, 1996), Matt. 10:14.
6. Ronald Reagan, *Reagan, in His Own Hand: The Writings of Ronald Reagan That Reveal His Revolutionary Vision for America*, ed. Kiron K. Skinner, Annelise Anderson, and Martin Anderson (New York: Free Press, 2001), 309.
7. "Quote of the Day," *Orange County Register*, March 6, 2004.
8. Reagan, *Reagan, in His Own Hand*, 426.

Index

About the Author

S teve Martin began his career programming computers as a teenager in the late 1970s. Through working with computers, he became acutely aware of the preciseness and structure of language. In addition, programming is built upon models—verbal descriptions and visual representations of how systems work and processes flow. Models enable repeatable and predictable experiences.

Early in his career, he was also introduced to the concepts of neurolinguistics, the study of how the human brain uses and interprets language. When he made a transition into sales, he realized that he could build models to create successful relationships based on customers' language and thought processes. Without any sales experience to speak of, he was the number one salesperson in his company for the following four years.

Steve went on to be a top sales producer for a billion-dollar company and was promoted into management to imprint his selling model on other salespeople within the organization. As vice president of sales, Steve successfully trained his salespeople on the sales strategies and communication skills that are necessary to close complex accounts.

Steve is the author of the critically acclaimed book about enterprise sales, *Heavy Hitter Selling: How Successful Salespeople Use Language and Intuition to Persuade Customers to Buy. Heavy Hitter Selling* is recommended reading by the Harvard Business School and has been featured in *Forbes* and the *Wall Street Journal*. The

Heavy Hitter Selling concepts have been studied by leading companies around the world, and Steve's sales training programs have
helped thousands of salespeople become Heavy Hitters.

Steve is also the author of *The Real Story of Informix Software
and Phil White: Lessons in Business and Leadership for the Executive
Team*. The book chronicles the meteoric rise of Informix Software,
how it became a Silicon Valley technology giant, and the scandal
that ultimately led to its spectacular fall.

A highly sought-after speaker, Steve is both entertaining and
provocative. He has made presentations to hundreds of companies
and organizations. Please visit www.heavyhitterwisdom.com for
further training and keynote speaker information.